The Papers of the Henry Luce III Fellows in Theology

Series in Theological Scholarship and Research

The Papers of the Henry Luce III Fellows in Theology
Christopher I. Wilkins, Editor

The Papers of the Henry Luce III Fellows in Theology

VOLUME V
Christopher I. Wilkins, Editor

ats Series in Theological Scholarship and Research

The Association of Theological Schools in the United States and Canada
Pittsburgh, Pennsylvania

The Papers of the Henry Luce III Fellows in Theology

VOLUME V

edited by
Christopher I. Wilkins

Copyright © 2002 by The Association of Theological Schools
in the United States and Canada

Library of Congress Cataloging in Publication Data

The papers of the Henry Luce III Fellows in Theology / edited by Christopher I. Wilkins
   p. cm. — (Series in theological scholarship and research)
ISBN 0-7885-0297-2 (alk. paper)
ISBN 0-9702-3461-9 (alk. paper) vol. V
1. Theology. I. Henry Luce III Fellows in Theology. II. Series.
BR50.P24 1996
230—dc20   96-27815
                              CIP

Printed in the United States of America
on acid-free paper

To Martin E. Marty

This volume is dedicated to Martin E. Marty in honor of his service as Chair of the Advisory Committee for the Henry Luce III Fellows in Theology program from 1994 - 2001 and for his continuing inspiration to the program.

Acknowledgment

The Association of Theological Schools expresses its profound appreciation to The Henry Luce Foundation, especially Henry Luce III, John W. Cook, and Michael F. Gilligan, for their generous support of the Henry Luce III Fellows in Theology program, the annual Luce Conference, and this volume.

Contents

Contributors to this Volume

Christopher I. Wilkins
The Association of Theological Schools

Susan R. Garrett
Professor of New Testament
Louisville Presbyterian Theological Seminary

Kathleen J. Greider
Associate Professor of Pastoral Care and Counseling
Claremont School of Theology

Margaret M. Mitchell
Associate Professor of New Testament
University of Chicago Divinity School

Larry L. Rasmussen
Reinhold Niebuhr Professor of Social Ethics
Union Theological Seminary

Don E. Saliers
Parker Professor of Theology and Worship
Candler School of Theology of Emory University

Susan E. Schreiner
Associate Professor of Church History and Theology
University of Chicago Divinity School

Nicholas P. Wolterstorff
Noah Porter Professor of Philosophical Theology
Yale University Divinity School

Introduction

Christopher I. Wilkins, Editor
THE ASSOCIATION OF THEOLOGICAL SCHOOLS
PITTSBURGH, PENNSYLVANIA

What follow in this volume are papers by specialists in theological education, written for the general reader. They are bound together in witness to the achievement of their authors—each of whom was a Henry Luce III Fellow in Theology in 1998-1999—and by something like serendipity. The papers have no necessary relation to one another, and yet have much to teach when read together. That is why they are bound in a single volume under the auspices of this program, although indexed separately in the relevant databases as well.

The Henry Luce III Fellows in Theology Program of The Association of Theological Schools in the United States and Canada, was begun in 1994 to support excellence in scholarship in all disciplines within theological education. Seven Fellows, each of whom must be a full-time faculty member at an ATS accredited or candidate school, are selected annually. Each Fellow receives support for a twelve-month sabbatical in which to conduct a research and writing project that is likely to be significant in its field. In addition, Fellows' projects are meant to bear good fruit to the academy at large, to communities of faith, and to the wider public—academic, faithful, or otherwise.

To write within one's chosen field is, at least, to master the relevant discourses, primary and secondary sources, styles, questions, modes of reference and allusion, and the inclusions and exclusions by which the field maintains itself within academic discourse. One cultivates one's field so that it may bear a good harvest, and eyes keen to tell wheat from tare in such a harvest never seem to close. However, to write for those outside that field lets one share the fruits of that harvest broadly and freely. One writes in this other way not to justify one's field or one's work in it, but to share what one has learned, allowing outsiders to make of it what they will.

It will be easy to see that the seven papers collected in this volume represent separate, and at times incompatible, fields of discourse. The claims made on our attention and future *praxis* by Larry

Rasmussen's analysis of eco-theism and faith communities' response to the needs of the earth do not read easily beside Nicholas Wolterstorff's immersion in Thomistic psychology and the precision with which God may or may not be said to feel your (or any) pain. In turn, the assumptions governing both their works challenge, and are challenged by, the techniques of dubiety and certainty Susan Schreiner draws from reformers, skeptics, and playwrights of the sixteenth century. Yet the questions all three papers raise about human limitations, self-knowledge, certainty, and the roles played in and upon human life by the natural and divine things that are not human resonate much more richly for being asked within each other's hearing.

Likewise, the careful homiletic, intellectual, and devotional attention that Margaret Mitchell finds John Chrysostom bringing to the life and writings of the apostle Paul at first appears unimaginable for those who suffer the psychospiritual trauma Kathleen Greider examines, or for those who care for, and about, them. Yet, holding these two papers together in one's mind shows that they elicit a common, crafted empathy. Which enables patient attention to those who come through knowledge but then linger in wisdom. Their experiences and lessons have much to teach, and rarely teach easily. Similarly, the questions Don Saliers poses to Christian liturgy with regard to beauty, holiness, and the roles they might play in contemporary society may helpfully be raised to each of Susan Garrett's presentations of angels. She notes several ways in which one's expectations of angels (or of their absence) shape how one can experience them. These, in turn, have much to teach those who would speak of beauty or holiness at all, and who would live and worship in light of what such experiences reveal.

These are only a few reflections that emerge from reading in succession the papers in this volume. If there is a theme common to them, it might well be trepidation before, and celebration within, human capacities and limitations. But finding a common theme is not essential. We invite you to read these papers together and judge them for yourselves. We hope that their unnecessary relation will reveal unexpected insights when you do.

According to Horace Walpole, to whom we are indebted for the word "serendipity," the three princes of Serendip "were always making discoveries, by accidents and sagacity, of things they were not in quest of . . . ." *"Serendip"* by itself, derived from the Persian and Arabic terms for Sri Lanka, connotes none of this. Yet the term abides in English in its own way, somewhere between chance and design and with its own lessons for invention, as the action not of the island, but of its imagined princes.

Whether the Fellows' discoveries parallel the princes' we leave to the reader to decide. It is enough for the ATS to have made something like such a discovery with this program since it began. The happy accident that brings the Fellows' works together each year inspires researchers involved in theological education to see their work in light of their plural vocation as scholars and as teachers. This vocation involves educating persons who, typically, are preparing themselves for ministry, the academy, or in response to a like calling. It is hope that this volume, like its predecessors, contains lessons that are of value to those who teach in this way, and to their students. We also hope that the work of the Henry Luce III Fellows in Theology in years to come, whether shaped by accidents and sagacity or not, will be likewise inspiring.

Angels at the Dawn of an Age

Susan R. Garrett
LOUISVILLE PRESBYTERIAN THEOLOGICAL SEMINARY
LOUISVILLE, KENTUCKY

Introduction

I s this all there is? These bodies that can be injured in the blink of an eye—bodies that grow sick, that die? These jobs or schools or friends or spouses that sometimes excite and challenge us but often do not? These unceasing worries about money or job or health or children or relationships? Is this all there is? Or is there another place, another dimension to life?

These questions are as old as humanity. Some of the most ancient and most enduring answers to them are found in the Bible, in both the Hebrew Scriptures or "Old Testament" and in the New Testament. Biblical authors take it for granted that there is a realm called "heaven." In that realm God sits in glory, with other divine beings surrounding the throne. Biblical authors assume, moreover, that the heavenly realm is near to our hands and hearts. Heaven intersects with earth at key places and key moments in the life of the people of God. At such key moments God's heavenly messengers, God's celestial soldiers, and at times even God venture forth from heaven to work and to be seen upon the earth. Jacob witnessed such an intersection of heaven and earth in his dream at Bethel: "He dreamed that there was a ladder set up on the earth, the top of it reaching to heaven; and the angels of God were ascending and descending on it. . . . And he was afraid, and said, 'How awesome is this place! This is none other than the house of God, and this is the gate of heaven.'" (Genesis 28:12, 17)

Questions about the connections between heaven and earth may be very old, but they are as pressing today as they have ever been. How else can we explain the phenomenal rise of interest in angels? It scarcely needs to be said that the evidence for this interest is displayed everywhere: on television, in book stores, in films, on the Internet, in women's magazines and in magazines devoted solely to the topic of angels, in *The New York Times*, on jacket lapels, in gift catalogues, and in greeting card stores. Researchers have developed sophisticated explanations for this deep and widespread interest, and these explanations have merit.[1] But whatever the large-scale trends or cultural pressures may be, on an individual level the topic of angels commands attention *because people want to know if there is more to life than meets the eye*. Those who believe in the reality of angels—and some of those who do not—are answering this question with a resounding "Yes!" They are saying that the world is not limited to what we can touch or taste or measure or record on videotape.

This new enthusiasm for heavenly affairs contrasts with attitudes that prevailed only a few decades ago. In 1970, sociologist Peter Berger observed, "Whatever the situation may have been in the past, today the supernatural as a meaningful reality is absent or remote from the horizons of everyday life of large numbers, probably the majority, of people in modern societies, who seem to manage to get along without it quite well."[2] Perhaps Berger overestimated the disdain for the supernatural felt by people at that time. But even if he did overestimate, clearly in the intervening decades perceptions of the otherworldly have changed. Many have left the sterile, self-contained, predictable world of late-1960s "modern man" far behind. They have found that the world again teems with angels and other spirit-beings, who are reintroducing elements of magic and surprise into their lives. Angels and their fallen counterparts are again alive and well! In a mere three decades we have witnessed the re-enchantment of the world.

Do Angels Exist, and What Counts As Evidence?

People who believe in the existence of angels can scarcely ever convince those who do not believe, and vice versa. The parties to the debate cannot persuade one another because they cannot agree about what should or should not count as evidence for angels' reality. Should biblical stories about angels count as evidence—or should they be dismissed as reflecting an outmoded worldview? Should a modern person's claim to have encountered an angel be tallied as evidence? If so, then what historical, visual, or psychological details are necessary to make such a claim persuasive? For example, if a person sees nothing unusual but alleges to have *felt* a spiritual presence, does that count? ("What you call an angel let me call nervous calm," wrote Goethe to Lavater.[3]) What personal or psychological factors would automatically discredit a person's claim to have had an angelic encounter? Or should *all* such claims be disbelieved, since another (this-worldly) explanation can nearly always be found?

The difficulty in knowing what to count as evidence stems from disagreement about where to begin the investigation. The people who argue with one another about angels' reality begin from different starting points—and then inevitably move on to different outcomes. Their preconceptions shape their experiences; their experiences, in turn, confirm their preconceptions. For example, on the one hand, conservative Christian defenders of angels (such as Billy Graham) often take the biblical accounts of angels as their starting point.[4] They then point to testimonies of people who claim to have encountered angels. The testimonies are taken to verify not only that angels exist, but also that angels' behavior and actions today resemble their behavior and actions in biblical times. *But the testimonies themselves do not reflect impartial experience.* Rather, Scripture has already informed and shaped the testifiers' very perception of angelic presences in the world.

On the other hand, as heirs of the modernist era, many "liberal" Christians take as their starting point their conviction that the world is largely barren of so-called supernatural powers. The cosmos is the sterile world described by Berger in the quotation given above. Not surprisingly, the experience of such Christians conforms to their expectations. In other words, their experience is shaped from the outset by their conviction that all (or at least all lesser) supernatural beings have been extinguished from the world—discredited as the figments of an earlier, more mythological day. Biblical accounts of such beings are then reinterpreted as metaphor or else moved to the outermost margins of faith. But contradiction can arise, for often the very same Christians who reject belief in gods, angels, demons, and the devil leave God (and perhaps the Holy Spirit) standing at the center of their beliefs—even though the same discrediting arguments could be applied to God/the Spirit as to the lesser beings.[5]

Finally, consider the case of the so-called New Age defenders of angels. They are the authors and readers of many of the angel-books to crowd the bookstore shelves in recent years. Such people have typically rejected the barren-world theory of scientific modernism. They begin instead with what we might call an "enchanted-world cosmology." At the outset they assume the world to be filled with spiritual presences and inexplicable powers. Predictably, such people then experience the world as filled with spiritual presences and inexplicable powers. It is not hard for such people to find "heaven's gate." They need only turn inward, or sit before a blank computer screen with mind open, or before a blank paper with pen in hand. Then, immediately, the angels of God begin to descend to make their presence felt and their wisdom known.[6] But, as with the other groups considered above, *such persons' experiences are suspect.* They are suspect because the experiences have been fundamentally shaped by the persons' prior expectations.

So we see that different presuppositions about the world produce different sets of angel experience. I do not point this out so as to discredit "conservatives," "liberals," or "New Agers," whom I freely admit to having caricatured here. Neither do I intend to raise up a new, fourth way to study angels—a way that will somehow escape the pressure-mold of its own premises. The point, rather, is that *everyone* comes at the topic of angels with certain assumptions already in place. Moreover these assumptions are not about picayune affairs. They pertain to the very biggest questions of life: Does God exist? If so, what is God like? Does God speak to humans? If so, by what means, and what sorts of things does God say? What is the nature of reality? Are there natural laws, and can they be broken? What is our human nature?—and so on. Miraculously, children learn to speak without any formal study of grammar. And so also each of us comes to assume certain answers to these and similar questions, even if we have never given them conscious attention. The answers we give to these questions in turn predispose us to perceive the world (with its "supernatural" elements—or lack thereof) in certain ways. Such bias cannot be escaped, for it is built into the process of all human knowing. We cannot "know" the world unless we have words and concepts and mental maps to "know with." But our words and concepts and mental maps shape and direct all that we perceive and how we make sense of it. We need not lament this built-in bias to all human knowing, but we do need to acknowledge it. Having recognized that there always is a bias, we can direct our efforts to tracing its contours in a given instance and discerning its effects on thinking about angels.

We learn our "mother tongue" at our parents' knees. And so also we absorb many of our key opinions about God and about the world from our parents, our family of origin, and especially from the larger culture (or sub-culture) in which we live. It can be difficult for us to see our own opinions because we are so close to them. The effort can be like trying to get a good, critical look at oneself without a mirror. What we need is a place where we can stand, to look upon ourselves and see how we and our assumptions fit into the bigger picture. We can procure such a vantage point by comparing our views to the views held in other cultures. Whenever anthropologists immerse themselves in the life of another people, they embark on a process of learning *two* cultures: their hosts' culture and their own. By "trying out" the words, concepts, and mental maps that another people uses to make sense of the world, the ethnographers come to better understanding of their *own* words, concepts, and mental maps. Perhaps we can gain the footing needed to see our own culture's governing assumptions about angels by immersing ourselves in the world of biblical angels and the authors who wrote about them. In other words, looking into the strange world of biblical angels may enable us to discern more clearly what is distinctive about various modern views of messengers divine.

Angels in the Biblical World

Often we think we already know what the biblical sources say. We may assume that the ancient accounts and our modern beliefs about angels are more or less consistent. For example, in the book *Angels* Billy Graham presupposes that his own view of angels matches "the biblical view." (Graham further takes it for granted that there is only one "biblical view.") As a second example, in Frank Peretti's several sagas about angels battling demons, the novelist assumes an identity between the angels he depicts and biblical angels. But in fact modern authors (and those who read their works) hold many ideas about angels that are quite foreign to the world of the Bible and vice versa.

Recent popular studies of angels—even those of the "New Age" variety—do often give passing attention to the biblical portraits of angels. But such works inevitably fail to offer the painstaking attention to detail and to exhibit the kind of historical expertise and critical judgment that are necessary to make the biblical texts yield their riches on this topic. Moreover, as if the challenges posed by the biblical accounts were not enough, much important information about ancient angel-beliefs is hidden away in other, more obscure ancient texts. Consider, for example, the difficult writing known as *1 Enoch*. This document has an extraordinarily rich angelology. But *1 Enoch* is preserved in its entirety only in Ge'ez, the language of ancient Ethiopia. We are at the mercy of the handful of scholars who have mastered this arcane tongue. Further, *1 Enoch* evolved over a period of time (roughly between the third century B.C.E. and first century C.E.) and had multiple authors and editors. It is full of gaps, repetitions, and inconsistencies. Even short passages by a single author are written in a style that can be very hard to follow. The challenges posed by *1 Enoch* and other such documents must be met, however, for there are crucial aspects of ancient Jewish and early Christian angel-beliefs that can scarcely be understood apart from them.

Biblical authors—like authors today—use stories about angels to talk not only (and not even chiefly) about angelic existence but about a whole range of subjects. The quest for understanding will be the most successful if we turn our eyes and ears to those other matters. Rather than focusing always on the question of angels' existence, it could be useful to try to discover *what else* was being said and heard when ancient authors wrote about angels. What were such authors claiming about God? About God's interventions in the corporate life of God's people? About God's interventions in the lives of individuals? About human sinfulness, human perceptiveness, human ability or inability to affect the natural course of events? And so forth. The specific questions would have to vary with the text in which a given angel account is found.

Bracketing the question of angels' existence is an important step in the search for understanding. By leaving the question of angelic existence open, we keep our minds open to discover new, metaphorical dimensions of truth in stories of angels. We thereby avoid that modern tendency in reading texts to "analyze, reduce, and narrow down toward definition." Writing of heaven, Jeffrey Burton Russell observes:

> Moderns are used to dichotomies between true and false, fact and fiction, they are put off by comparative terms such as 'more real' or 'more perfect,' and they create a dichotomy between 'literal' and 'metaphorical'…The modern assumption is that the so-called factual statement relates to 'outside reality' and that the metaphorical statement is subjective and unrelated to 'outside reality.'[7]

But because of their vastness and richness, some realities—including heavenly realities—*cannot* be conveyed or grasped except through metaphor. Biblical authors sensed all this. "God is a poet at least as much as a scientist or a historian," Russell writes.[8] The truths that biblical authors sought to convey in their descriptions of angels overflow the words and images at those authors' disposal. If we seek to discover the "metaphorical" or "poetic" truth of their descriptions, we are not prejudging the question of angelic existence. We are not saying that angels "aren't real, but only metaphorical." Rather, we are declining to focus on the (finally unprovable) issue of their reality or non-reality, in an effort to discern the larger meanings of stories that tell about them.

As an illustration of the point, consider the prophet Isaiah's awesome vision of "the Lord sitting on a throne, high and lofty":

> In the year that King Uzziah died, I saw the Lord sitting on a throne, high and lofty; and the hem of his robe filled the temple. Seraphs were in attendance above him; each had six wings: with two they covered their faces, and with two they covered their feet, and with two they flew. And one called to another and said, "Holy, holy, holy is the Lord of hosts; the whole earth is full of his glory." The pivots on the thresholds shook at the voices of those who called, and the house filled with smoke. And I said, "Woe is me! I am lost, for I am a man of unclean lips, and I live among a people of unclean lips; yet my eyes have seen the King, the Lord of hosts!"
>
> Then one of the seraphs flew to me, holding a live coal that had been taken from the altar with a pair

> of tongs. The seraph touched my mouth with it and
> said: "Now that this has touched your lips, your guilt
> has departed and your sin is blotted out." Then I
> heard the voice of the Lord saying, "Whom shall I
> send, and who will go for us?" And I said, "Here am
> I; send me!" (Isaiah 6:1-8)

Here Isaiah uses human words and images—instruments of limited capability—to describe an encounter so rich with meaning as to defy description. What words could ever suffice to portray an encounter between infinite God, the creator and Lord of the universe, and a weak, fallible, fragile human being? Or what words could express the marvelous truth that a mortal was selected to stand in God's presence and carry God's word to the people? In choosing his words and images, Isaiah was not writing a neutral, objective description of events, the way a lab worker might write up an observation report for an experiment whose outcome does not deeply interest him. Rather, Isaiah was describing an experience of being overwhelmed by God—an experience in which the prophet was not detached observer but full participant. Inevitably, that experience surpassed the capacity of the words and images that Isaiah chose to convey it.

And yet, the prophet's words and images are what are left to us. So we proceed to translate and to unpack and to explicate. We envision the scene in our mind's eye, and we ponder the symbolic import. Likely we will all agree that the account is at least partly symbolic. Surely Isaiah's lips were not physically burned—but just as surely he was purified somehow, so that his mouth should be enabled to speak God's holy words. But how much else in Isaiah's account has symbolic or metaphorical import? What about the throne? What about the seraphs? What about the wings of the seraphs? It doesn't get us very far simply to say that the seraphs were or were not "real." It is much more fruitful to ask what their presence as God's attendants, or their covering of their own eyes, or their purifying act means for Isaiah's overall depiction of God's majesty. *We need to fix our attention on precisely such questions of meaning.*

We always speak to one another—and God always speaks to us—in particular languages. These "languages" encompass more than just words. They encompass entire cultures—the fantastically complex sets of symbols, assumptions, practices, and mental maps shared by a given people. To understand what is being said and heard in a given act of communication we need to know (or rely on someone who knows) the relevant language and the relevant culture. Consider Isaiah's vision once more. The words of the vision can be translated readily enough, but we quickly realize that more is needed for understanding. For example: (1) What does it mean to say that God sits on a "throne"? To answer, we need information about the understandings and practices and accoutrements of kingship—not kingship in the twenty-first century, or the sixteenth century, but kingship in the days of "King Uzziah" (eighth century B.C.E.). Otherwise we will read later ideas of thrones or of kingship back into the earlier text. (2) Who or what are "seraphs"? Are they angels such as we normally think of angels today? Then how is it that they have six wings instead of two? Here again knowledge of Isaiah's culture helps us to grasp the scene: "seraphs" (or "seraphim") were winged serpents, often depicted in Ancient Near Eastern (especially Egyptian) art in association with royal thrones. (3) Why do the seraphs cover their faces? Yet again, knowledge of the culture (specifically of biblical culture) assists us: by biblical convention, God is so holy that no one can see the face of God and live. By covering their faces the seraphs call attention to that extreme holiness: even these supernal creatures cannot look upon God's face. No wonder the mortal Isaiah cried "Woe is me!" The point is that biblical authors were influenced as much by *their* culture as modern authors are by modern culture. In order to maximize our understanding of angels—whether they be biblical angels or angels of the twenty-first century—we need to view the depictions of them against the backdrop of the relevant culture. Only by doing so can we perceive nuances of the accounts and also minimize the reading of our own cultural assumptions into them.

When we view ancient depictions of angels in their cultural context, we come upon ideas that seem outmoded or strange or mysterious to us. Consider, for example, the widespread assumption in the Ancient Near East that the stars, sun, and moon are living beings. Biblical authors adopt this assumption, depicting celestial bodies as part of "the heavenly host," who fight in God's angelic army against the enemies of Israel. As the author of Judges writes, "the *stars fought from heaven*, from their courses they fought against Sisera" (Judges 5:20).[9] Or, consider Paul's statement that women should wear head coverings "because of the angels" (1 Corinthians 11:10). What could he possibly mean? Here it would be helpful to have still better knowledge of Paul's culture than what we do possess. From his culture Paul has apparently adopted certain assumptions—obscure to us now—about the role of angels in worship or else about the behavior of angels toward women (or both). Is it possible, as some have suggested, that Paul supposes the angels will be sexually attracted to the sight of the women's uncovered heads? (We do know that the story of angels who mated with human women, told in Genesis 6:1-4, was widely known and discussed in the first century.) Whenever we come upon such strange and mysterious elements of ancient angel-beliefs we should note them well. They will remind us not to get too comfortable with the biblical stories—not to assume that we always know exactly what the ancient authors were talking about. Even when ideas look familiar, authors may be making assumptions and associations that we cannot understand or accept.

As the word of God, the Bible comes as a gift to us. But it is a book authored by humans who lived in worlds radically different from ours. We are always, in very important ways, foreigners to it. We therefore approach it best with sensitivity and respect. Consider the story of two outsiders who go to live in a small village in another country. One is loud and demanding. She insists that residents meet her needs and relate to her in the manner to which she was accustomed in her own land. The other outsider is gentle and respectful. He takes months or years to get to know the residents of the village and to understand their ways. He learns from them far more than the first visitor can ever learn, for he is receptive to wisdoms other than ones which he has always known. We face similar options as we foray into the biblical world of angels. We can barge in, demanding that the biblical authors support our preconceived views. Or we can look, listen, and learn. If we choose the latter course, what we see and hear may be rather different from what we expect.

But the situation is more complicated than the above story suggests, for the Bible is not a village whose inhabitants all know one another and all share, more or less, the same perspectives. The books of the Bible were written by different people from different cultures over a span of many centuries. Hence the authors present *various* ideas—about angels and about other topics, too. Sometimes these ideas are simply different from one another, and sometimes they seem actually to contradict one another. As an example, consider again the issue of the "heavenly host." When Isaiah writes of the starry host, he portrays it as fully subordinate to God from the beginning:

> Lift up your eyes on high and see: Who created these? He who brings out their host and numbers them, calling them all by name; because he is great in strength, mighty in power, not one is missing. (Isaiah 40:26)

But in another passage, members of the host are set to be judged by God, suggesting that they have strayed from God:

> On that day the LORD will punish the host of heaven in heaven, and on earth the kings of the earth. They will be gathered together like prisoners in a pit; they will be shut up in a prison, and after many days they will be punished. Then the moon will be abashed, and the sun ashamed; for the LORD of hosts will reign on Mount Zion and in Jerusalem, and before his elders he will manifest his glory. (Isaiah 24:21-23)

In this passage the host is *not* depicted as fully in harmony with the divine will, but as a gathering of independent gods who oppose the LORD. So the LORD will punish them (along with their earthly counterparts, the rebellious human kings). Many modern authors who survey biblical angels simply ignore such tensions in biblical depictions of the heavenly host or individual members of it. They assume that all scriptural teachings are consistent; what is said of angels in one part of Isaiah can be used to shed light on what is said in another part; what is said in Genesis can be used to shed light on what is said in Hebrews, and so forth.[10] Another option, though, is to strive to hear *all* the different voices in scripture—whether they be harmonious or dissonant. With respect to the example given above, many biblical scholars contend that Isaiah 24:1–27:13 (from which the second passage above is taken) was written by another author working a hundred years or more after the eighth-century prophet Isaiah of Jerusalem (who authored the first of the two passages cited). The two authors' ideas about the host differ because their own backgrounds and the purposes for which they wrote differed.[11] When we harmonize their teachings on this topic we flatten and reduce their respective words to us. But when we strive to pick out the different voices speaking in Scripture and hear each voice in its own context we produce a richer interpretation and we better respect the integrity of the authors and first readers of the biblical texts.

Some of the most exciting recent discoveries in the study of ancient beliefs about angels pertain to the figure of Jesus. Immediately after Jesus' death his followers mined biblical and other textual traditions for imagery and language that could explain Jesus' identity and the nature of his reconciling work. Scholars are finding evidence that some important traditions that Christians adapted for this purpose were *traditions about angels*. These included especially various traditions about a chief angelic mediator or "right-hand angel" to God. We see the evidence of "angelic Christology" scattered throughout the New Testament, but one of the most striking instances occurs when Paul recalls the welcome that the Christians in Galatia extended to him when he first preached to them the Gospel. Paul writes, "[T]hough my condition put you to the test, you did not scorn or despise me, but welcomed me as an angel of God, as Christ Jesus" (Galatians 4:14). Commentators usually assume that Paul means his statement hypothetically: "You welcomed me as warmly as you would have welcomed an angel of God—indeed, as warmly as you would have welcomed Christ Jesus himself." But there is good reason to suspect that Paul is claiming that the Galatians received him "as God's angel—namely, Jesus Christ." In other words, Paul is making the startling claim that when he first preached the Gospel to the Galatians, he was united with Jesus Christ (cf. Galatians 2:20), whom Paul identifies with God's chief angel. In other passages, too, Paul's language suggests that he made sense of Jesus' person and work *by likening him to angels*, or even by *identifying him with the chief angel of God*. Other New Testament authors did the same, including the authors of Luke and Acts, the Gospel of John, Hebrews, Jude, and Revelation.[12]

In the early Christian view, then, it is Jesus and no ordinary angel who is the truest and best messenger from God. It is Jesus who has most perfectly revealed God's identity and God's intentions for the created world. But Jesus differs from the angels in one all-important respect: he suffered and died. Moreover, that suffering and death are not incidental to the message that Jesus brings, but are its very heart. Yet, in comparing Jesus to the angels the early Christians did not simply pit him against them, for they presumed that he is like them in quite important ways. So also any comparison today between Jesus and the angels can never be a simple matter of our showing his superiority to them. We must also explore to find what he and they have in common.

Angels As They Were and Are

A look in bookstores or search on the Internet will quickly reveal that modern angels fill various job descriptions. They are healers, guardians, givers of praise. They are soldiers fighting for God against their fallen counterparts—namely, the devil and the demonic hordes. At the hour of death they are guides who lead humans to "the other side." Biblical or other ancient depictions of angels lie somewhere behind most of these modern ideas about angelic roles. It would be fascinating to trace the lineage of these various ideas as they pass through the 2000 intervening years of the Common Era, but to do so would be an enormously complicated endeavor requiring a multivolume work. Still, even if we cannot trace how this or that notion of angels evolved through the centuries to come to its present manifestations in culture, we can benefit from looking at the ancient counterparts to modern notions and vice versa. Such a strategy may permit a clearer perception of how *each* such image— be it ancient or modern—functioned (or functions) within its own social, historical, and theological contexts.

It is hard to know which of the recent representations of angels to treat. On the one hand, it might seem to make sense to limit study to testimonies by people who claim that they have encountered angels or to have special wisdom about them. These testimonies are found on the Internet, in various published collections and magazines, and in the burgeoning number of angelic "self-help" books offering advice on how to make contact with angels or tap into their power.[13] In such cases the narrators at least purport to tell the truth. So their accounts might seem worthier of our attention than the openly fictitious depictions in recent print, drama, film, and television. But the "fictional" accounts must be treated also, for they exercise enormous influence on the popular imagination. David Ford comments on the huge audiences for films and videos, and on the millions of readers of novels:

> They are being drawn into a fictional world, and in turn are welcoming fictional people and plots into their lives. This is something of immense importance. Taking part in this fiction-saturated culture, we discover who we are and we test our identities. We enter into the fictional world of novels, plays, films, and all sorts of other stories. But the lines between fiction and reality are not at all clear, and our hopes, fears, dreams, and conceptions of reality may be more profoundly affected by fiction than by "true stories" (if those are what historians and journalists tell).[14]

The millions of people who have watched *Touched by an Angel* each week have been stirred in ways that will affect millions more. So also with the millions who have seen Frank Capra's classic film *It's a Wonderful Life,* or the millions who have seen the other, more recent angel-films, or the millions who have read Frank Peretti's apocalyptic novels about angels battling demons.[15] So, it might prove fruitful to compare and contrast both types of modern angelic representations—the "fictional" and the "non-fictional"—with biblical portrayals that correspond in some way.

The distinction between the "non-fictional" and "fictional" accounts of angels turns out to be quite a slippery one in any case. The testimonies that people offer are "fictions" also—even if the reported events really happened. As much as television-script writers and movie producers, those who testify to encounters with angels "make" or "create" their accounts. They do so by choosing which elements of the encounter to report and how to narrate the story so as to elicit the most sympathetic response from readers or hearers. When one reads the testimonials, it quickly becomes apparent that the narrators' choices on such matters follow established conventions. For example, many accounts of miraculous angelic intervention in a time of crisis end with the disappearance of the "mysterious stranger" who gives the aid. He or she simply vanishes. No one, however, ever actually witnesses the disappearance, the way Alice witnessed the disappearance of the Cheshire cat. Rather, the narrator is typically distracted for a moment, and when he or she turns to say "thanks," the stranger is gone. Later efforts to track the "angel" prove fruitless. The "disappearance of the angel" is a nearly indispensable feature of the modern genre of angelic-encounter narratives. Narrators of such stories have been influenced not only in their narration of such experiences *but even in their initial perception of them* by what they themselves have seen and heard in other, earlier such testimonies—not to mention what they have seen and heard in the fictional media depictions, or what they have read or heard from the Bible.[16]

In all times and places, talk of angels points to a reality beyond that which we can see. When people today talk of angels, they are implicitly asking or asserting something about such a transcendent reality. Just *what* they are asking or asserting can vary greatly. For example, when people tell stories of guardian angels who rescue them from impending disaster, they are claiming that a higher power (Christians would say "God") watches over them and guides their steps. Or, when people tell stories of "healing" angels who "open blind eyes," they are claiming that there is a liberating truth for each of our lives, a truth that can be sought and found. To give yet a third example, when people tell stories of "fallen angels" causing destruction and mayhem, they are claiming that life is not what we envision for ourselves—nor what God envisions for us. Given that the questions and issues underlying "angel talk" are of such magnitude, any serious effort to interpret biblical or modern angel accounts must probe deeply. It will not do to treat them casually, or mockingly, or without attention to the difficult matters posed by our own linguistic or cultural distance from them. When we do approach such stories with all due respect, they will tell us a great deal indeed—about God, and about ourselves.

Endnotes

1.   See Robert Wuthnow, *After Heaven: Spirituality in America Since the 1950s* (Berkeley: University of California Press, 1998).

2.   Peter L. Berger, *A Rumor of Angels: Modern Society and the Rediscovery of the Supernatural* (Garden City: Doubleday, 1970), 5.

3.   Quoted by Karl Barth, *Church Dogmatics* (Edinburgh: T. & T. Clark, 1960), 3, part 3, 377.

4.   Graham writes, "I believe in angels because the Bible says there are angels; and I believe the Bible to be the true Word of God" (*Angels: God's Secret Agents* [Reprint edition; Dallas: Word Books, 1994], 15).

5.   The dismissal of all notions of "mythological," interventionist powers came with the transition to modern forms of discourse in the Enlightenment. Theologians of the modern era have typically sought to explain what exists and what transpires in creation by referring, not to transcendent realities, but only "to what is also in and of the world according to principles manifested by the visible intra-worldly connections of proximate and particular causes" (Kathryn Tanner, *God and Creation in Christian Theology: Tyranny or Empowerment?* [Oxford: Basil Blackwell, 1988], 125). Thus, in the twentieth century, the works of modernist theologians such as Rudolf Bultmann and Paul Tillich reflect their efforts to construe God's presence and care in a "non-mythological" way, in keeping with the truths of the scientific age. Bultmann wrote, "Modern men take it for granted that the course of nature and of history, like their own inner life and their practical life, is nowhere interrupted by the intervention of supernatural powers" (*Jesus Christ and Mythology* [New York: Charles Scribner's Sons, 1958], 16; see also 20-21). But Bultmann and Tillich endeavored to construe *all* supernatural powers (including God/the Holy Spirit) non-mythologically, and therefore did not fall into the kind of self-contradiction referred to above. In today's (postmodernist) era, many theologians reject the modernist conviction that it is even possible to speak "non-mythologically," holding instead that we never escape the grip of our own "mythological" constructs, though we may substitute one set of conceptual models for another. In *God and Creation*, Kathryn Tanner argues compellingly against the modernist framework, insofar as it forces us to choose between a construal of divine powers as transcendent to the created order and a construal that emphasizes God's immanent presence. Such a framework is responsible, Tanner argues, for the incoherence of much modern theological discourse about God's ongoing role vis-à-vis creation: for the modernists, God's radical transcendence excludes God's creative operation within the world. Rather, Tanner argues, God must be described "non-contrastively" as both radically transcendent *and* radically immanent.

6.   See, e.g., Ambika Wauters, *Angel Oracle: Working With the Angels for Guidance, Inspiration, and Love* (New York: St. Martin's Press, 1995); Alma Daniel, Timothy Wyllie, and Andrew Ramer, *Ask Your Angels* (New York: Ballantine Books, 1992); Barbara Mark and Trudy Griswold, *Angelspeake: How to Talk with Your Angels: A Guide* (New York: Simon & Schuster, 1995); Eileen Elias Freeman, *Touched By Angels: True Cases of Close Encounters of the Celestial Kind* (New York: Warner Books, 1993).

7.   Jeffrey Burton Russell, *A History of Heaven: The Singing Silence* (Princeton: Princeton University Press, 1997), 7.

8.   Ibid., 9.

9.   John J. Collins observes that in the Ancient Near Eastern world stars were not viewed as inanimate objects but were "the visible manifestation of the heavenly beings" (*Daniel: A Commentary on the Book of Daniel* [Minneapolis: Fortress Press, 1994], 331).

10.   This assessment applies to Billy Graham, *Angels*; also Duane A. Garrett, *Angels and the New Spirituality* (Nashville: Broadman & Holman, 1995), esp. 10-26. A more sophisticated evangelical treatment of angels in the Bible is that of Stephen F. Noll, *Angels of Light, Powers of Darkness: Thinking Biblically about Angels, Satan, and Principalities* (Downers Grove: InterVarsity Press, 1998).

11.   On the use of an Ancient Near Eastern myth in Isaiah 24:21-23, see Theodore H. Gaster, "Host of Heaven," in *Encyclopaedia Judaica*, 16 vols. (New York: Macmillan, 1971-72), vol. 8, 1046. On the difficulty of dating the so-called "Little Apocalypse' of Isaiah (chapters 24-27), see William R. Millar, "Isaiah 24–27 (Little Apocalypse)," *The Anchor Bible Dictionary*, 6 vols. (New York: Doubleday, 1992), 3: 488-90.

12.   The preceding analysis of Galatians 4:14 is based on Charles A. Gieschen, *Angelomorphic Christology: Antecedents and Early Evidence* (Leiden: Brill, 1998), 315-25. See ibid., 315-51 for treatment also of other passages in Paul's epistles.

13.   See works cited in n. 6 above. Best-selling testimony collections include Sophy Burnham, *A Book of Angels: Reflections on Angels Past and Present and True Stories of How They Touch Our Lives* (New York: Ballantine, 1990); Joan Wester Anderson, *Where Angels Walk: True Stories of Heavenly Visitors* (New York: Ballantine, 1993); see also the periodical *Angels on Earth*, which is published by Guideposts and consists almost entirely of stories of angelic intervention.

14.   David F. Ford, *The Shape of Living: Spiritual Directions for Everyday Life* (Grand Rapids: Baker Book House, 1998), 34.

15.   Frank E. Peretti's novels include *This Present Darkness* (Wheaton: Crossway Books, 1986), and *Piercing the Darkness* (Wheaton: Crossway Books, 1989). The reader reviews of Peretti's works at the Amazon.com website are revealing of the power and influence the works have had for many readers.

16.   Wuthnow writes of the "legacy of spirituality within congregations and families that supplies the underlying models for these experiences" (*After Heaven*, 115). His chapter "Angel Awakenings" (in ibid., 114-141) gives an insightful overview and sociological analysis of the recent boom of popular interest in angels.

"Dark" Nights of the Soul: Meaning and Ministry in First-Person Narratives of Severe Psychospiritual Suffering and Healing

Kathleen J. Greider
CLAREMONT SCHOOL OF THEOLOGY
CLAREMONT, CALIFORNIA

Prelude

Throughout his adulthood, the writer of the following passage suffered episodes of psychosis, depression, and psychiatric hospitalization. For most of his life, he was employed as a chaplain to psychiatric patients, teacher of seminarians, and seminary professor. His first profession, however, was forestry, and the anecdote he relates in the passage comes from that period of his life.

> I often think of a little incident which occurred when I was in Washington. One of the old Forest School men had just returned from two years in the North Woods and a lot of his old class-mates were gathered around him while he dished out yarns about his experiences in the wilds. Finally one of the men asked, "Say, Bill, have you ever been lost?" Bill straightened up, glared at him, and replied with some heat: "Lost! Of course I've been. It's only the dubs who never go five miles from camp who don't get lost sometimes."
>
> I agree with Bill. The kind of sanity which has to be preserved by sticking close to camp and washing dishes for the rest of my life is not worth preserving. I could never be happy or contented in such a course, especially when I feel that the particular territory in which I lost my way is of greatest interest and importance. I want to explore and map that territory.[1]

This young man's first job—forestry—became a metaphor for his vocation—mapping the terrain of sanity and insanity amid religious belief and practice. Analysis of the text reveals insights as well as unanswered questions. Insanity is not romanticized theologically or otherwise—it is hell. Neither, however, is sanity idealized—the only ones who *never* get lost are the "dubs" who "stick close to camp." Feminist analysis helps us see just how dull the dubs are: the storyteller has them stuck with a fate normally ascribed to females—washing dishes for the rest of their lives. The storyteller emphasizes the "heat" in Bill's response, perhaps because it conveys that "have you ever been lost?" is an irritatingly naïve question to pose to a forester just returned from two years in the wilderness. Bill's reply suggests that getting lost is part merely of *finding* the "territory . . . of greatest interest and importance," much less exploring and mapping that territory. Moreover, it is precisely the fact that someone has been lost in the wilderness and lived to tell about it that can capture the public's attention and turn his stories into "yarns." Disappointingly, however, the author does not unearth from the metaphorical anecdote an answer to the question that, for non-foresters, is arguably the most intriguing one: what kind of person takes a job that requires two years alone in the North Woods and lives to tell about it? Theologically, religiously, spiritually—what "possesses" such people?

The writer of the passage is Anton Boisen, who from 1938-1942 was a full-time member of the faculty at Chicago Theological Seminary and whose book *Exploration of the Inner World* is still considered an important contribution to the literature in the field of psychology of religion.[2] Boisen is most widely known as the founder of "CPE"—the now-international clinical pastoral education training program for seminarians and other religious caregivers. Most important for the purposes of this essay, however, is Boisen's contribution to method in pastoral theology, care, and counseling. As the Bible is a primary text for biblical scholars, and classical documents are primary texts for historians and theologians, so the primary text for pastoral theology and care is what Boisen called the "living human document"—the dynamic text of human-being-in-community. Boisen's formulation voiced a long-standing hermeneutical challenge in the study of the primary texts of pastoral theology and care: unlike most other scholarly texts, living human documents literally talk back to the pastoral theological scholar and fluctuate right before the scholar's eyes. Moreover, for sophisticated com-

prehension of the texts of their discipline—the lives of human beings—pastoral theological scholars' comprehension of the texts of
their own lives is prerequisite.

Rationale, Resources, and Methods for the Project

Persons who survive severe psychospiritual suffering, or accompany a loved one through such turmoil, hover at the margins of
theological discourse and religious community. By "severe
psychospiritual suffering" I refer not only to psychiatrically diagnosable conditions but also to any emotional experience and expression, whether understood psychologically or spiritually, that
causes acute and persistent anguish and interferes to some degree
with one's ability to function appropriately in one's contexts. While
persons who suffer from psychiatrically diagnosable conditions are
arguably the most severely marginalized, most cultures discrimi-
nate and, usually, segregate, a wider range of emotional experience
and behavior as extreme and inappropriate. Furthermore, while
the marginalization of persons and families afflicted by severe
psychospiritual suffering is arguably most rigorous in Western societies, it is increasingly a global problem.

More and more, however, especially in the U.S., these persons
and families are producing public, autobiographical narratives of
their suffering and healing: books, poetry, media interviews, con-
gressional testimony, and video documentaries. In these texts, those
with personal knowledge of severe psychospiritual suffering and
healing offer description of the phenomenology of their experience,
analysis of its cultural (religious, sociopolitical, economic, racial,
gender, etc.) significance and, importantly, exploration of issues that
are either explicitly or arguably theological, religious, and/or spiritual. While today their experiences tend to be understood primarily
as mental illness, their texts regularly nuance a more complex reality, what ancients referred to as the "dark night of the soul." Unfortunately, superstitious and racist connotations still attributed to
darkness obscure its value to the soul, and contemporary people
tend to see in severe psychospiritual suffering little more than unnecessary and treatable pain. In contrast, first-person narratives
of severe psychospiritual suffering make clear—without romantici-

zation—that nights of the soul are comprised both of senseless pain and of kairotic moments of insight and joy, moments craved and yet seldom known by the psychiatrically healthy majority. In short, first-person narratives of severe psychospiritual suffering and healing offer intriguing and unexplored insights for theological discourse, religious communities, and spiritual maturity.

My research for the 1998-99 Henry Luce III Fellows in Theology program has entailed pastoral theological study of substantial samplings of this genre of unique and heretofore largely unexamined texts—narratives produced by persons and families suffering from mental illness and other forms of severe psychospiritual suffering, especially privileging accounts that explicitly or implicitly raise issues of theology, religion, and/or spirituality. The analysis above of the Boisen passage—an excerpt from an autobiographical account of severe psychospiritual suffering and healing—serves as example of both the method and data of my research project. I have analyzed approximately 125 book-length autobiographies and numerous shorter, written memoirs by survivors or their families and friends. Additionally, I have examined about two-dozen first-person video accounts and had countless conversations with survivors of severe psychospiritual suffering. Since the narratives are predominately but not exclusively Christian in orientation, the project has yielded ecumenical and, to a lesser degree, interreligious perspectives on these questions.

The project is organized through utilization of three primary methodological approaches common to pastoral theology, care, and counseling. By treatment of the Boisen text and other first-person narratives excerpted for this report, these methods are demonstrated. First, the method of clinical case study is obviously central. Analytically considered anecdotal human experience is assumed to have heuristic value through the revelation of particular truths that good scholarship neither disregards nor universalizes. The study also follows method in the construction of feminist and other liberation theologies: fuller understanding of acute psychospiritual suffering and healing is constructed by bringing expert persons outside the immediate experience into collaboration with "base-communities," those who have first-hand experience of such suffering and healing. Finally, it utilizes narrative theological methodology, where insight for theology, religion, and spiritual development is constructed from what can be identified as "true to life." Following Lucy Bregman's and Sara Thiermann's approach to the study of first-person narratives,[3] the study is not hagiographical but analytical—it seeks to comprehend both constructively and critically the meanings, limitations, and values imputed to severe psychospiritual suffering and healing by persons who have first-hand experience of it.

The remainder of this essay presents findings from the five research questions that have structured my inquiry. Given the necessity for brevity here, the discussion of each research question is an excruciatingly cursory overview of the range of responses I have found. Somewhat more substantive treatment is given to issues that have particular relevance to a primary emphasis in the Henry Luce III Fellows in Theology program—the theological and public dimensions of the projects.

Research Questions

Research Question 1: As described by persons who have survived their own severe psychospiritual suffering or that of a loved one, what are the significant causes, qualities, and dynamics of the turmoil?

Pain is personal and particular. Still, common themes addressing the causes, qualities, and dynamics of severe psychospiritual suffering emerge across the range of first-person descriptions. In the excerpt from Boisen, we encountered a characterization that is both common and theologically significant: severe psychospiritual suffering is commonly called "hell." It is tempting to defuse this characterization by treating it as merely metaphorical. To do so is theological folly, though, since these narratives relentlessly enumerate evidence that the concept of hell may indeed name an actual dimension of human suffering and not either a mere metaphor or a future threat. In the experience of severe psychospiritual suffering, "hell" is less a place of the soul's possible punishment after death and more the everyday and endless pain of a psychospiritually sick soul with no hope that suffering will ever end *except*, ironically, in death. Excruciating *physical* pain can have this effect, though in narratives of severe *psychospiritual* suffering, "hell" frequently has a distinctive torment: the *illnesses themselves* often cause afflicted ones to feel that they are elementally corrupt, in contrast to being unfairly or accidentally wounded. Science has proven that many sufferings once explainable only as demonic possession or deserved divine punishment are in fact disorders of the brain or treatable emotional disabilities. Nonetheless, the non-rational sense of wrong-doing and self-blame is a common symptom or side effect of psychiatric illness. For many people living with the often invisible, still-mysterious, soul-betraying symptomatology of severe psychospiritual suffering, every day is "judgment day."

The daily faultfinding is not only internal, however. Another dominant theme in descriptions of severe psychospiritual suffering is that of stigma: specifically, the pain of the stigma inflicted on persons suffering mental illnesses and other forms of severe psychospiritual suffering is said to be worse than the suffering itself. Almost without exception first-person narratives of severe psychospiritual suffering are extensively occupied with what Susanna Kaysen calls "stigmatography," the charting and describing of the stigma associated with being identified as mentally ill.[4] Lutheran scholar and ordained clergyperson Stewart Govig, father of a son diagnosed with schizophrenia, says that human societies are infected with "mentalisms," prejudices akin to racism, sexism, and classism.[5] Persons and families who cannot hide their psychospiritual distress are at risk of being judged categorically weak, dangerous, and repellent. Another reason that the stigma is often more destructive than the suffering itself is because, in the social-psychological dynamics of oppression, it is nearly impossible for persons stigmatized not to internalize the marginalization and subordination, not to stigmatize themselves, not to feel self-hatred and shame.

A third common characterization of the suffering centers on the enormity and the incomprehensibility of the losses suffered by persons with psychiatric illnesses and other forms of severe psychospiritual suffering. Some losses contribute to the causes of madness, many are side effects of illness, others are the costs of stigma, and a few are coincidental. Whatever loss's role, the narratives are testimonies to the anguish of loss. Poignantly, the spiritual and material poverty considered so foundational on the pathway to saintliness is common and concrete in severe psychospiritual suffering: these narratives detail loss of material possessions and employment, loss of vocation and purpose, loss of hope and faith, loss of relationships and shared dreams, loss of innocence and illusions of control, loss of belief and/or religious community. Most foundationally chronic and severe psychospiritual suffering is characterized by the loss of one's sense of—or even capacity for—agency and power. These sufferers are repeatedly deflated, pricked by actual social disempowerment but also, since they are constantly buffeted by immersion experiences in the real existential limits of human power, by an intermittent leaking away of their feeling of personal authority.

Constantly confronted with the limits of their agency and capacity to influence, it is not surprising at all—though many comment upon it with amazement—that religiosity tends to increase both helpfully and unhelpfully in persons suffering severe psychospiritual turmoil. It seems obvious from these narratives that religiosity increases among sufferers because it offers access to power. Religion, spirituality, and theology—talk about God—are fundamentally concerned with ultimate questions about power in sacred and in evil manifestations: What power creates life? What power nurtures life? What power undermines life? What power ends life? When the personal agency, relational connections, and social status are lost, concern for the power of life and death moves center stage.

Unarguably, the most prominent common theme regarding the causes, qualities, and dynamics of severe psychospiritual suffering is that it has multiple causes, and its resolution requires multiple remedies. Scientists' quickly expanding knowledge of genetic, neurological, and structural origins of psychiatric illnesses and some other forms of severe psychospiritual suffering is invaluable, both for expanding treatment options and for undermining stigma. In an interesting parallel to advocacy strategies that emphasize genetic and neurobiological theories of homosexuality in order to destigmatize it, mental illnesses are increasingly referred to as "no-fault disorders of the brain." First-person accounts provide critical balance, however, because they make indisputable the complex interaction of neurobiology, environmental traumas, and social disorders in the causation of severe psychospiritual suffering.

A video narrative recorded by "R.B." in the docudrama "Dialogues with Madwomen"[6] emphasizes how R.B.'s eventual disintegration into a state resembling dissociative identity disorder is complexly and cumulatively a part of a "matrix of miseducation"—racism, sexism, poverty, and violence. This articulate African American woman's narrative is an ocean of troubled waters: race-based marginalization, sexual assault at the hands of an acquaintance who calls her "goddess," homelessness and, as we will explore later, moralistic and racist formulations of Christianity. Her narrative also reveals the interplay of personal agency and lack of control in the experience of severe psychospiritual suffering: she takes responsibility for "tak[ing] the lid off," and then adds in the passive voice that "the bottom was falling out."

If R.B.'s suffering is symptomatic, not only of the functioning of her brain, or the idiosyncrasies of her personality, or neglect or trauma in her upbringing, but of chronic social sicknesses, then scientific reductionism offers the cheapest of grace. From a pastoral theological perspective, science's single-gene theories and "silver-bullet" medications are clearly partial diagnoses. If care for severe psychospiritual suffering leads only to treatment of the disordered brain, potentially more life-threatening diseases of the soul will be masked and allowed to spread. Severe psychospiritual suffering will take the rap for damage done not by biochemistry alone but by the human capacity for doing harm and evil. This is yet another form of blaming the victim and allows the interpersonal violence and social injustice underlying much severe psychospiritual suffering to go unchallenged. Moreover, medical or other scientific theories of single causation, however compelling, will always be partial answers and are unlikely ever to be sufficient to satisfy human souls worn ragged at the intersection of disordered societies, interpersonal cruelties, personal limitations, and existential suffering.

Research Question 2: What do narratives of severe psychospiritual suffering reveal as major theological, religious, or spiritual issues and questions?

First-person narratives of severe psychospiritual suffering offer "thick descriptions"[7] of theological, religious, and spiritual dilemmas. Several themes emerge that have particular relevance to the theological and public dimensions of severe psychospiritual suffering. Not surprisingly, perhaps, is that the oldest and most persistent theological question abounds in these texts: Does (a) God exist? Is there a Creator, Supreme Love, Higher Power, Ultimate Purpose, Core Value? This endlessly debated theological issue appears explicitly or implicitly in most narratives of severe psychospiritual suffering, even in narratives where religious affiliation is disavowed or no other theological or spiritual concerns are identified.

Almost as common are questions about God's role in severe psychospiritual suffering: Where is God in relation to my suffering? Why is God allowing this to go on? Is God doing this to me? Why is God doing this to me? Is there anything I can do to get God to stop? These kinds of questions—and the range of possible answers to them—are constrained by the most common image of God. Biblical and theological assertions that there exists a God that is simultaneously loving, omnipotent, and omniscient are especially confounding to persons suffering chronic psychospiritual anguish. Certainly, throughout Christian history, some people in severe psychospiritual suffering have made their peace with this theology: affirming that God is good, all-knowing, and all-powerful comforts some persons with the affirmation that their suffering has meaning and purpose, even if obscured or heartbreaking. In these narratives, however, there is evidence that significant numbers of persons in severe psychospiritual suffering and their families are alienated from formal religious affiliation and practice precisely because they experience such theology as inadequate, irrelevant, or inhumane. Even communities that profess belief in a god imaged as suffering-with-us not infrequently operationalize a different theology, especially in prayers. Implied contradictions abound, for example, when a community espouses a suffering god and also implies God's omnipotence through intercessions and thanksgivings for healing. A god credited with the power to heal can be argued to be accountable as well for healing's absence or for seeming favoritism in healing.

The inadequacy of moralistic and dogmatic interpretations of Scripture and/or religious doctrines forms another theme in these narratives. Persons and families of persons whose suffering has been shown scientifically to be caused by malfunctioning of the brain, ask: How am I to relate to religious texts and religious assertions that either demonize severe psychospiritual suffering or suggest that it results from a lack of character, determination, or devotion? Parents of a child suffering psychospiritually ask: How am I to relate to religious texts and religious assertions that children's suffering or well-being reflects mainly on the parents?[8] When others have given up hope for them, persons with chronic psychiatric disorders ask: With all that I have lost—children, spouses, friends, money, jobs, church communities, dreams—how am I to sustain hope? Given the extremity of my psychospiritual suffering, why and how should I go on living?

Indeed, this question leads us to the most common theological, religious, or spiritual issue in these narratives. Though many narratives of severe psychospiritual suffering are not explicit about any other theological, religious, or spiritual issue, the problems and possibilities of one issue—suicide—are present in nearly all. R.B.'s videotaped story, noted above, is illustrative. In the previous section, we noted the multiple causality in R.B.'s suffering—classism, racism, sexism, self-preservation, naïveté, violence at the hand of an acquaintance. After the assault, R.B. says, "I said to Life, if this is what I [can] expect of my species, I need another reason to stay here." Violated by a violence she does not simply project onto others but identifies with her own species, for R.B. "staying here" has become a question, is no longer assumed, not a requirement, maybe not even reasonable. The apparently growing rate of suicide among children and teens may signal that "staying here" is less reasonable than ever, given the violence that children are coming to expect of their species—other children. Years later, after dissociation and homelessness and poverty, R.B. is still trying to reason it out. She tells us, in a perfectly matter-of-fact tone, "I considered slitting my wrists, and so I said, well, why shouldn't I?"

> This was after I had earned my way home, and my family had gone out to a candlelight service for New Year's Eve . . . . They invited me and I couldn't imagine going to church where I had learned about all this blond God and blond Jesus with the blue eyes, and what did that have to do with me? And

that was part *of* the damage, and so I said "no thanks." So there I was, being the girl, washing the dishes on New Year's Eve in my mother's house. I'm 25, and I'm thinking: "Is this what I have to look forward to in life, to end up back here?"

Biblical and doctrinal prohibitions against suicide are either text or subtext of nearly every first-person narrative of severe psychospiritual suffering. Arguing from the fundamental theological assertion that life is a gift from God that a faithful person never spurns, religious prohibitions against suicide are largely inattentive to the experience of suicidal persons. Theological, ecclesial, and social prohibitions against suicide are remarkable for their power to eclipse compassion for persons who commit, attempt, or threaten suicide. Indeed, narratives indicate that, more than any other single factor, suicide and the taboos associated with it can divide the most loving family members from their afflicted loved one. Families often feel indicted by their loved one's suicide: What kind of love do we have if it doesn't prevent family members from killing themselves? Whole families are tainted by contact with the taboo of suicide and must choose between enduring the stigma and hiding the circumstances of their loved ones' death. Where persons succeed in committing suicide, it is legal to penalize their families; insurance companies must pay death benefits to families whose loved ones die in homicides, accidents, or any medical condition except fatal psychiatric illness.

In contrast to the bedlam of all these judgments, in first-person narratives there are still, small voices trying to explain what suicidal feelings are like. Psychotherapist and Episcopalian layperson Martha Manning offers one explanation in her account of suffering through a clinical depression that had been impervious to the battery of treatments levied against it. Amid the contradictions and paradoxes in this passage, Manning describes the spiritual dilemma formed by the demands of her coexisting compassion and suicidality.

> September 6, 1990 . . . .The aching relentlessness of this depression is becoming unbearable. The thoughts of suicide are becoming intrusive. It's not that I want to die. It's that I'm not sure I can live like this anymore . . . .

> I was always taught that suicide is a hostile act, suggesting anger at the self or others....But I think that explanation excludes the most important factor—suicide is an end to the pain, the agony of despair, the slow slide into disaster, so private, but as devastating as any other "act of God." I don't want to die because I hate myself. I want to die because, on some level, I love myself enough to have compassion for this suffering and to want to see it end.[9]

Research Question 3: What can be learned from these narratives about the processes of meaning-making and soul-sustenance in relation to ultimate values in the midst of severe psychospiritual suffering?

Spiritual, theological, and/or religious processes of meaning-making and soul-sustenance hold a prominent place in first-person narratives of severe psychospiritual suffering. Such resources are valued insofar as they comfort, impart meaning, connect to caring others, speak of hope in things unseen, nurture aliveness, or cooperate with sacredness. First-person narratives suggest several core processes that help make meaning and sustain the soul in severe psychospiritual suffering: formal religious practice, reliance on biblical literature, exposure to the aesthetic, cultivating a sense of gratitude, opening to everyday epiphanies, and, building a relationship to one's finitude.

For some authors, *material, organized religion* is helpful. Though often disparaged and discarded by healthy and healers alike, a variety of religious practices, objects, and communities make appearances in these accounts: rosary beads and prayers, crucifixes, meditation alone and in groups, Buddha chants, recitation of creed, intercessory prayer, charismatic groups, Bible studies, specters of saints and ministrants, retreat centers and retreats.

Even authors who disavow religious identity utilize *biblical literature's* special and enduring capacity to give voice to human suffering. Biblical images, allusions, and quotations are utilized in almost all narratives of severe psychospiritual suffering. Govig explains their use this way: biblical language "can both sharpen the pain and frame the heartache."[10] For example, I wonder if Martha Manning intended the Calvary-like allusion I perceived in parts of her description of her first electroconvulsive therapy (ECT) treatment: "I offer myself up to these strangers in exchange for the possibility of deliverance. . . .Fingers anoint my temples with cool ointment and fasten a plastic crown tightly around my head."[11]

The combination of severe psychospiritual suffering and the human hunger for meaning-making and soul-sustenance seem to yield a sense of perspective grounded in and expressed through recurring and thus irrepressible *humor*. Especially interesting for our purposes is humor that seems to aid processes of meaning-making and soul-sustenance. One example: Martha Manning relates a conversation about God with her sister, a recovering alcoholic, in which her sister observes that "religion is for people who are afraid of going to hell. Spirituality is for people who have already been there."[12] Manning, an active Episcopalian, seems to take pleasure in repeating this joke for her readers and thereby adding her agreement. While the religious mainstream can take offense at this comment, this irreverent humor helps distinguish spiritual exploration and expression from organized religion. Since organized religion and communities of faith so often fail people in severe psychospiritual suffering, spirituality can thus be redeemed and endure.

Exposure to the *aesthetic* is not simply pleasure, or privilege, or luxury, but lays the foundation for lifesaving moments. William Styron tells of being roused out of his most suicidal reverie and into the sanctuary of a psychiatric hospital by a soaring passage from Brahms's Alto Rhapsody, probably because, before his mother died when he was thirteen, he heard her sing it. Similarly, *Dialogues with Madwomen* dramatizes the role of the aesthetic in R.B.'s decision-making regarding life and death. The video text shows R.B. singing spirituals to ease her sense of exodus while in law school, dancing in the forest to cope with the sexual assault, and carrying a small harp even when she is homeless and mostly without possessions. These combine to suggest that the aesthetic is not optional but essential, life-giving in the face of death and other destructions. The climactic and closing moment of R.B.'s video narrative directly follows the excerpt quoted in the previous section wherein R.B. recounts that "I considered slitting my wrists, and so I said, well, why shouldn't I?" The video dramatizes that R.B. is distracted from slitting her wrists by lyrics and notes welling up internally. The words emerging in the music are an insistent, swelling chant: "thank you, thank you, thank you"—twenty times in all the mantra pulses. There is little of classic beauty in this aesthetic. This is the aesthetic of thunder, of a tsunami wave of primordial energy, of the barely communicable but incisive *gratitude* most of us know only in rare moments of ecstasy.

For what does a person in severe psychospiritual suffering have to be grateful? The hardship and isolation related in her narrative could evoke an understandably bitter response: "*Thank you*? Thank who? Thank who for what? Thank the builders of the matrix of miseducation, thank the underlings who carried out the violence, thank the church for damaged spiritual food? Thank life for bringing me to question why I should 'stay here'?"

The mantra pulses twenty times—"thank you, thank you, thank you"—and then ends abruptly with a succinct coda: "Thank you for today." The mantra "thank you for today" nudges R.B. toward *everyday epiphanies*, flashes of insight specially sized for meaning-making and soul-sustenance among people who have known too much violence and disappointment. Everyday epiphanies typically offer only a glimmer of hope, enough to arouse the curiosity of the suffering, not enough to arouse their cynicism. Everyday epiphanies make meaning and sustain the soul by sanctifying the kindness of even one person, revealing holiness through concrete substances, and thus reawakening awe for life. Martha Manning describes such an everyday epiphany during her efforts to recover from depression:

> After a morning of errands, I come home to find a bunch of tulips stuck in our mail slot ... without a note. They are breathtaking—a fiery red-orange opening to reveal the most incredible golden stars in their centers. Each time I catch sight of them, I am enthralled. I lose my focus, my balance. No matter what I'm doing, I have to stop and go over to peek inside to assure myself that the gold stars are still in there. They always are, and for a moment I let myself believe in God again.[13]

At closer examination, a double-meaning seems imbedded in the mantra: the thanks can go both ways, expressed by R.B. and

expressed to R.B. The voice is most clearly R.B.'s, expressing gratitude one day at a time. Understood spiritually, the voice may also
come, in part, from "beyond" R.B., and thus be an expression of
gratitude to R.B. for the contributions she makes to life: "Thank
you for today, R.B." Used in this way, the mantra helps cultivate a
sense of gratitude for every small and large thing not tainted by the
suffering. The mantra reiterates gratitude that even in the distress
of dissociation, R.B. can contribute from her "creative force in full
bloom." Over time, everyday epiphanies help build a *relationship to
one's finitude*. In severe psychospiritual suffering, the process of
meaning-making and soul-sustenance can do no other than refuse
the tendency of human nature—especially those of us lucky enough
to be temporarily-abled—to idolize health and well-being. Rather,
meaning is made and souls are sustained by living one day at a
time, by the glimmering light of partial understanding, in the mysterious co-mingling of suffering and joy. People who cultivate a sense
of gratitude while living one day at a time amid the severe
psychospiritual suffering associated with schizophrenia are exemplars of this kind of meaning-making and soul-sustenance. Schizophrenia dashed dreams in the Govig family and forced them to live,
unwillingly, within limits. It took years to find it, but therein was
embedded a remarkable salvation experience. "Eventually we . . .
managed to abandon a few of the cultural dictates of success. It was
then that we caught our first glimpse of the banks of Jordan."[14]
"Jordan" came in the form of a community devoted to the simple
skills and pleasures of daily living, the Pacific Community Mental
Health Center. Beyond the "cultural dictates of success," Govig and
his family found the grace of life within limits, and in the despised
limits, rediscovered God:

> Life within limits has become a vital reality and
> slowed down my pursuit of religious and
> psychological crutches. Anger recedes and the
> strangest reframing of all has taken place: rebirth
> within the boundaries of God's salvation . . . . It spurs
> a movement toward God.[15]

*Research Question 4: What do first-person narratives reveal about
positive and negative influences of religious communities and religious professionals in the midst of severe psychospiritual suffering?*

In contrast to the number of authors in this study who portray themselves as having either religious or spiritual identities and concerns, religious communities and religious professionals are strangely absent from these narratives. For example, Stewart Govig, who is a Lutheran clergyperson and implies that he and his family have a relationship to a local congregation and pastor, barely mentions the involvement of pastors or church in the family's struggle.[16] Due to increasing cultural secularization and the stigma attached to religiosity, it is reasonable to attribute the invisibility of religious communities and religious professionals partly to authors' hesitancy to publicly identify themselves as religious. Also, in situations where the psychospiritual suffering is due to psychiatric crisis, the absence of religious communities and religious professionals is due to the greater immediate priority of mental health care. In other cases, this absence is due to the paucity of resources provided by religious communities and religious professionals and to the higher value and magical hopes attributed to medical professionals: Govig admits that he and his wife "surrendered to professional expertise and ignored resources within . . . religious faith."[17] Despite his chronicle of psychiatry's inadequacies, Govig confesses that "I am still inclined to approach medical personnel like priests of healing whose words for Jay's illness become magical answers to the pain and dilemmas a parent such as I must face."[18]

Still, the absence of explicit religious care in these stories is also reflective of religious communities and their leaders being widely untrained and/or unwilling to engage with those in the grip of mental illness and many other forms of severe psychospiritual suffering. Govig criticizes the church for its lack of attention to and its silence about, both in prayer and education, the needs of the mentally ill and their families.[19] Pam Martin, an Episcopalian laywoman, observes that even when there are prayers for healing, churches may not distinguish between healing and cure, and judge and shun those whose illnesses do not yield to prayer.[20] By an uncritical reliance on the work of willing volunteers, without adequate attention to their nurture, churches may encourage the faithful in patterns of religious devotion that are ultimately self-diminishing: Manning implies that, early in her depression, her over-extension in congregational duties was a way to avoid consciousness of her symptoms. Frederick Frese—a psychologist, Roman Catholic, and person with schizophrenia—tells stories of two priests whose problematic actions are illustrative. During one paranoid episode, a priest gave him printed material about entering the priesthood. Few religious communities are prepared to assess when religiosity is inflaming severe psychospiritual suffering and not easing it. In other cases, the stigmatized behavior of persons in severe psychospiritual suffering so frightens some religious professionals and communities that they overreact with limit-setting: during another paranoid episode, Frese came forward during the Mass, uninvited but not disruptively, and knelt beside the altar, at which point the priest threatened to call the police if Frese did not leave the church.[21] At the worst, religious professionals and religious communities who keep their distance or offer facile judgments are seen as representatives of a harsh God.

More positively, it is some relief to learn from these narratives that nothing is more healing than simple human kindness, and that religious professionals and religious communities are, in more than a few narratives, exemplars of simple human kindness. Religious leaders and communities who even haltingly reach out to those brought low by severe psychospiritual suffering are received with notable grace and patience. While the value of aesthetic worship and social ministries are not to be minimized, even more valuable is the authentic humanness of a religious community and its leaders. In keeping with the value of everyday epiphanies in meaning-making and soul-sustenance, it is encouraging to learn from these narratives that religious communities and religious professionals can be helpful to persons in severe psychospiritual suffering in simple, non-engineered moments, through patience, aliveness, hope, and humility. When Anton Boisen was hospitalized in a psychiatric ward, his seminary friends were faithful through letter-writing and visits. In the midst of the routine of Sunday service, Martha Manning's imagination is captured by a priest's simple action: He reads the Gospel with "life and passion."[22] Pam Martin's spirit was empowered more than once in the most anguished moments of her family's struggle with depression by a congregation called Church of the Resurrection. She says that "the light" didn't move from the pulpit to the congregation but rather "rose from the people, arching to meet the altar."[23] Stewart Govig tells of everyday signs of hope seen through a minister who has spoken out about the needs of persons with chronic mental illness and provided teaching information so that churches can determine the best way to respond.[24]

R.B.'s video narrative illustrates the ambiguity—a tangle of negative and positive contributions—of religious leadership and community in severe psychospiritual suffering. R.B. soothes her soul with spirituals, the legacy of African American religious community. Unfortunately, she sings them alone and not in community. She is alienated. Because in her experience of the African American church, the church camouflages the spirituals' rebellion in the tradition, taught by religious leadership, of "a blond god and blond Jesus with blue eyes." The stage is set for R.B.'s contemplation of suicide when, feeling she had to protect herself from the values of her family's worshipping community, R.B. turns down their invitation to New Year's Eve services and falls into the despair of her isolation. Paradoxically though, R.B. relates in her narrative that as she fell further and further into severe psychospiritual suffering, she knew and trusted the legendary strength and care of the matriarchs of African American congregations: "I had a sense that I really needed help, one of these church mammas would materialize." When R.B. relates how an airport cleaning woman who took the homeless R.B. "under her wing" and a woman riding the bus expressed concern for R.B.'s bare feet, it hardly matters whether they are actually members of religious communities. Even though she has guarded herself against some of the teachings of African American Christian tradition, the traditions' "church mammas" have cultivated in R.B.'s soul a capacity to anticipate and accept the everyday epiphany of caring strangers.

Research Question 5: How do those who suffer mental illness and other severe psychospiritual suffering characterize authentic healing and effective care?

One of the primary themes in narratives relevant to this question is the necessity to distinguish between curing and healing. Precisely because of the interplay between neurobiological, social, and existential causation, severe psychospiritual suffering is rarely cured. While cure is so rare that it is often interpreted as miraculous, healing is not just possible but frequent and inspiring. Healing requires multiple remedies, and some forms of *therapeia* are mentioned more frequently than others in narratives of severe psychospiritual suffering.

It does not cure but is healing to admit to the mystery that pervades inner anguish. Psychospiritual suffering is "mysterious in its coming, mysterious in its going,"[25] says writer William Styron in an exquisite memoir of his depression. "To me," Stewart Govig offers, "mental illness carries an ultimate: it hints at the yawning, formless void present at the beginning before God's wind swept over and brought light to general disorder."[26] These narratives attest repeatedly to the limits of our knowledge: We do not know much at all about what causes this suffering, why it afflicts this person and not that one, why now and not then. Styron speaks with appreciation of the honesty of a clinician who used this analogy to describe human understanding of severe psychospiritual suffering: "If you compare our knowledge with Columbus' discovery of America, America is yet unknown; we are still down on that little island in the Bahamas."[27] Extending the analogy, survivors of severe psychospiritual suffering and their loved ones are disregarded natives, well-versed in living amid both the fruits and the difficulties of wilderness, at risk of colonization instead of collaborative community.

It does not cure but heals to give oneself over to the simple pleasures of life, even those found within the unavoidable limits of severe psychospiritual suffering. Govig offers a poignantly illustrative vignette of giving himself over to the well-being found in the child-like silliness sometimes exhibited by his son who suffers from schizophrenia. He and Jay go together to a buffet-style restaurant. "As usual, . . . silence reigned in our booth until all of a sudden my dinner companion ventured, 'Have you seen someone slurp Jell-O?'" When Govig's reply is no, "with a furtive glance about to make sure no one was looking, Jay lifted a couple of Jell-O cubes, and 'slurped' them through his lips. I was awarded a broad toothless grin." Throughout his account, Govig tells us that he is often embarrassed by his son's behavior. But in this situation he seems overcome with affection for his son and relief at this respite from torment and says, simply, "I could not help joining his simple mirth."[28]

Another common characterization of the process of healing in the face of severe psychospiritual suffering is that it often is found, paradoxically, in the depths of despair. The phenomenon of "hitting bottom," so well known in processes of healing from addiction, appears as well in narratives of healing in situations of severe psychospiritual suffering. While steps do need to be taken to insure the afflicted one's physical safety, family and other loved ones are often too protective, too soon. Sometimes "hitting bottom"—letting down one's persona, whatever behaviors our cultural context prescribes as being consistent with sanity—is part and parcel of movement toward healing. While it does not cure, "bottoming out" is often exactly the circumstance that focuses one's attention, clarifies priorities, and motivates one to get on the path toward accepting help and healing.[29] Important to mention because it flies in the face of stigma and stereotypes is the example of psychiatric hospitalization. Some persons who have experienced severe psychospiritual suffering, especially (though not exclusively) those with the insurance and other financial resources to buy the best psychiatric care, testify that they found healing sanctuary in some psychiatric hospitals. Looking back on his hospitalization and recovery, Styron says that, "For me, the real healers were time and seclusion."[30] Hospitalization is always difficult and never a cure in itself. Some persons are hospitalized too quickly, for too little reason,[31] and others have told tales of harrowing incarcerations under horrible conditions.[32] Still, though they are usually and understandably overshadowed by accounts of horrific experiences in psychiatric hospitalization, persons with psychiatric illnesses speak of the need for quietness and a place of retreat. In such times, hospitalization can have value.

It cures nothing but is powerfully healing when the suffering ones are able to make a contribution to the lives of the healthy majority and thus make concrete the purpose and value of their living. Manning is moved to tears when, even as she is struggling with depression, her therapist affirms her abilities by referring a client to her and when friends insist that they were really hoping that she, not her husband Brian, would baby-sit their children.[33] Similarly, the most common rationale stated by authors of first-person narratives of severe psychospiritual suffering for revealing their personal lives is their hope that the story might help others similarly afflicted.

R.B.'s video narrative illustrates one additional contribution to healing processes, and that is the healing power of unsentimental presence. We can identify unsentimental presence in the interactions between R.B. and the two women who functioned for her as church mammas. We get only a glimpse of their interactions with R.B., but note what R.B. remembers of their words to her: "Baby, you OK?" "Where your shoes, girl?" At first their care is nonverbal: they *see* R.B., they do not look past or through her. They see R.B.'s circumstances—she is sleeping in an airport restroom, she is without shoes. Thus, they see not only R.B.'s circumstances, they see R.B. *in* those circumstances and this moves them to offer her affection and concern. In the way she tells the story, what seems most memorable and significant for R.B. is presence, not mawkish posturing but unsentimental matter-of-factness. Throughout its history, pastoral theology and care has called religious professionals and religious communities to exactly this art. These two "church mammas" make this ancient, fine, rare art look easy.

Conclusion

Anton Boisen claimed that the territory of the "wilds"—what we have been calling severe psychospiritual suffering—is of greatest interest and importance for pastoral caregivers, students of religion, and other people of faith because religion is *responsible* for some soul-sickness and, at the same time, an indispensable part of *healing* some soul-sickness. Religion plays roles in both the causes and "mapping" of psychospiritual wilderness.

After telling the anecdote about old Bill, related at the beginning of this report, Boisen goes on as follows:

> Sanity in itself is not an end in life. The end of life is
> to solve important problems and to contribute in
> some way to human welfare, and if there is even a
> chance that such an end could best be accomplished
> by going through Hell for a while, no man worthy of
> the name would hesitate for an instant.[34]

Boisen's overall view of severe psychospiritual suffering and healing offers some touchstones on which to close this essay. "The end of life"—its purpose and goal—is not sanity or insanity. Rather, the purpose and goal of life is the solving of important problems and making a contribution to the common good. Boisen's life and work are evidence that insanity can be a pathway to such problem-solving and human welfare. A radical value is thereby asserted and modeled: "If there is even a chance" that the common good might be served in the hell of insanity, the person worthy of being called human does not cling to sanity. While these narratives make excruciatingly clear that severe psychospiritual suffering is romanticized only by the naïve,[35] they *all* also speak of its value.[36] In and through their suffering, the authors of these narratives find the sacred, have moments of profound tenderness with others, grow in their appreciation of everyday pleasures, and see through the sham of many dominant values.

Endnotes

1. Anton T. Boisen, *Out of the Depths: An Autobiographical Study of Mental Disorder and Religious Experience* (New York: Harper and Row Publishers, 1960), 132.

2. Anton T. Boisen, *The Exploration of the Inner World: A Study of Mental Disorder and Religious Experience* (New York: Harper, 1936). For a complete bibliography see Glenn H. Asquith, Jr., ed., *Vision From a Little Known Country: A Boisen Reader* (Decatur: Journal of Pastoral Care Publications, Inc., 1992).

3. Lucy Bregman and Sara Thiermann, *First Person Mortal: Personal Narratives of Dying, Death, and Grief* (St. Paul: Paragon House, 1995).

4. Susanna Kaysen, *Girl, Interrupted* (New York: Turtlebay Books, 1993).

5. Stewart D. Govig, *Souls Are Made of Endurance: Surviving Mental Illness in the Family* (Louisville: Westminster John Knox Press, 1994), 89. Citing William Anthony, Mikhal Cohen, and Marianne Farkas, *Psychiatric Rehabilitation* (Boston: Center for Psychiatric Rehabilitation, 1990), 20, 28-29. It is widely acceptable in the dominant culture—in this context, the so-called mentally healthy majority—to make jokes and use disrespectful language ("nuts," "crazy," "loony," "batty," etc.) about persons with mental illness and other forms of severe psychospiritual suffering, and it is done by people who would never make such jokes about race or gender, or other forms of disability.

6. Allie Light and Irving Saraf, producers, Allie Light, director, *Dialogues with Madwomen*, 90 minutes, 1993. For further information contact Women Make Movies, Inc.

7. Clifford Geertz, *The Interpretation of Cultures* (New York: Basic Books, 1973), 3-30.

8. Pam Martin, *Touch the Angel's Hand: A Family's Struggle with Depression* (Oak Park: Meyerstone Books, 1988), 30; Govig, 7-8. Govig cites Deut. 5:9 for example: "I the Lord your God am a jealous God, punishing children for the iniquity of parents. . ."

9. Martha Manning, *Undercurrents: A Therapist's Reckoning with Her Own Depression* (San Francisco: HarperSanFrancisco, 1994), 99.

10. Govig, 83.

11. Manning, 124.

12. Ibid., 178.

13. Ibid., 167.

14. Govig, 50.

15. Ibid., 84.

16. Ibid., 44.

17. Ibid., 46.

18. Ibid., 89.

19. Ibid., 48, 81.

20. Martin, 52.

21. Frederick J. Frese III, "A Calling," *Second Opinion* 19 (January 1994): 17, 20.

22. Manning, 16.

23. Martin, 53.

24. Govig, 92-93.

25. William Styron, *Darkness Visible: A Memoir of Madness* (New York: Vintage Books, 1992), 73.

26. Govig, 83.

27. Styron, 11. See also Manning, 58-59.

28. Govig, 90.

29. Govig, 39.

30. Styron, 69.

31. Kaysen, 7 ff., 39 f., 40, 71.

32. For a contemporary account of this type, see Kate Millett, *The Loony-Bin Trip* (New York: Simon & Schuster, 1990).

33. Manning, 73-74 and 146-147.

34. Anton T. Boisen, *Out of the Depths*, 132.

35. See, for example, Manning, 173.

36. See, for example, Govig, 95.

His Most Devoted Interpreter: John Chrysostom and the Art of Pauline Interpretation

Margaret M. Mitchell
UNIVERSITY OF CHICAGO DIVINITY SCHOOL
CHICAGO, ILLINOIS

Chrysostom's Portraits of Paul

In my Luce Fellowship project I sought to engage in an investigation into the craft of biblical interpretation through a special focus on the art of Pauline exegesis and exposition as practiced by John Chrysostom (ca. 349-407), the apostle Paul's most devoted and prolific patristic interpreter.[1] In his homilies on the Pauline epistles (more than 250 of them), and throughout his massive oeuvre, the fourth-century Antiochene John's obsession with the person of Paul leaps off the page. His hermeneutics is robustly and unapologetically author-centered. John claimed that he understood Paul so well, not because of his own mental acuity, or even his steadfast faith, but because he loved him so much, and "constantly cleaved" to him.[2] John's exegetical work enshrines this "love hermeneutics" wherein the favored saint (an *aoratos philos,* "invisible friend")[3] is best understood by those who meet him in love, to whom he directly communicates the truths of his writings. As John himself expressed it:

> I love all the saints, but I love most the blessed Paul,
> the chosen vessel, the heavenly trumpet, the friend
> of the bridegroom, Christ. And I have said this, and
> brought the love which I have for him out into the
> public eye so that I might make you, too, partners
> in this love charm.[4]

We shall start our analysis, not with a text, but with an image, from a twelfth-century psalter and odes manuscript now in the National Library in Athens (*Athen.* 7, fol. 2; see Plate 1).[5] This stunning color image is one of the best extant examples of the standard iconographical representation of John and Paul together. But to understand the image one needs to know the legend upon which it is based. In the seventh century George of Alexandria, one of John's

Plate 1: Photograph by Leonidas Ananiades, used with permission of the National Library, Athens.

biographers, tells the following tale about John and Paul. When John was patriarch of Constantinople, he chose to live in simple, ascetic means. In his semi-monastic cell he had a writing desk and copy stand, and a portrait of St. Paul on the wall. As he intently read Paul's letters, John would carry on conversation with the picture on the wall as though it were alive, by turns asking assistance in understanding from the author, and praising him for his amazing skill. As John was composing his homilies on the Pauline epistles, his secretary, Proclos, happened to peer in the door at the right moment (three nights running!) and witnessed a man standing over John's shoulder whispering exegetical hints into his right ear. He later identified the man for his master (who had been unaware of any unusual occurrence) by pointing at the picture on the wall and exclaiming: "the man I saw speaking with you looked just like this. Indeed, I think it *is* he!"[6] This legend puts into narrative form the substance of Isidore of Pelusium's earlier, famous remark, that "if the divine Paul had taken up the Attic tongue to interpret himself, he would not have done it differently than this renowned man has done."[7]

The manuscript illustration in this Byzantine codex (Plate 1) enshrines the legend in what was to become the standard iconographical depiction of John and his beloved Paul. John sits in the familiar philosophical or didactic pose, at his slanted writing desk. On the wall of his room the picture of Paul is highly visible, and yet simultaneously Paul stands, alive and embodied, peering over John's shoulder in the pose of a muse, as he composes his homilies on the apostle's letters (the matching facial features and color scheme of the garments make the identification of the picture with the standing figure unmistakable). The nimbi of the two saints intersect, creating a single halo that encloses the two heads. The faces of the two men are themselves quite similar, with broad foreheads (though Paul's beard is more prominent). In the doorway to the right one can perceive the shadowy presence of Proclos, who attests to the nocturnal visitation that authenticates John as Paul's definitive interpreter. This miniature beautifully captures the hermeneutical dynamics of Pauline interpretation as John carried it out. Paul's dual depiction in the miniature as simultaneously a frozen icon and a living, breathing and speaking presence demonstrates the genuine interpretive ambivalence John faced and described in studying Paul's letters. He was acutely aware of the absence and distance of the apostle in the present, the inability to "see" him now, yet he also felt that in touching the codex,[8] in hearing the apostle's words read, and in studying them carefully and preaching on them, he was in constant, lively conversation with him.

> Continually when I hear the letters of the blessed Paul read . . . I rejoice in the pleasure of that spiritual trumpet, and am roused to attention and warmed with desire because I recognize the voice I love, and seem to imagine him all but present and conversing with me.[9]

In his homiletical-exegetical art John sought to introduce, indeed, to bring to life, the Paul whose living voice he heard in the reading of his letters. To effect this "reading of resuscitation," John composed portraits of his saintly author—verbal portraits of Paul's body, of his soul, and of the episodes of his life. When read in the light of contemporary Greco-Roman literature and rhetorical theory, it becomes clear how much these literary portraits are cast in well-known ancient rhetorical forms (and would have been understood as such by their rhetorically attuned audiences). In my project I have analyzed John's portraits of the apostle Paul not only as expressions of his personal piety (though they are that), but as carefully crafted compositions that are part of a deliberate rhetorical strategy for Christian catechesis and social formation in the Christian imperium of the late fourth century.

John's portraits of Paul constitute a type of creative literary mosaic. They draw upon the biblical sources of the letters and the Acts of the Apostles, but reconfigure and recast them in the forms of Greco-Roman pulpit rhetoric. Pauline interpretation as John practices it is not a depersonalized, neutral endeavor in which a person (the reader) meets an object (a written text), but rather is a conversation among friends. In awakening Paul from his grave to speak to contemporary audiences and to be paraded forth as an example of piety before their eyes, the orator-exegete always has a contemporary end in view. John's portraits of Paul were directed toward the sculpting, the fashioning of Christian lives in imitation of this "archetype of virtue," both as individuals and as a *polis* founded, not on the customary activities of civic unification, such as the assembly, the theatre and the games, but upon a laicized version of the monastic virtues.[10] John recognizes that he is involved in a "culture war" of sorts, when he complains that people know inside and out the names and biographical details of the actors, actresses, and jockies (*Celebrity Digest* or *People Magazine* fare), but do not even know the names of the cities to which Paul wrote![11]

Yet even as John was seeking to form the late-antique Christian society in Paul's image, he was casting Paul in the hues of his own life, which was itself consciously and deliberately lived in imitation of his hero. He viewed (and lived) his own life in Pauline terms, even as he saw in Paul an image of himself. So, for example, John the monk, who left the life of a hermit behind after two years to return to ecclesial ministry in the city, portrays his Paul as the quintessential urban, "worldly" ascetic.[12] And John, writing in Antioch when the emperor Julian's pagan revival was still a living memory, casts Paul as the antitype of Julian, as the apostle who singlehandedly overthrew the institutions and monuments of Greco-Roman paganism and persuaded the whole world to join the one "true" philosophy. Like himself, John portrays Paul as a reluctant, yet stunningly effective orator who exercises his prowess only by the power of the spirit within him. Life, art, and exegesis are inseparably intertwined in this mimetic dance; symbiotic engagement with the author is an essential ingredient of the task of biblical interpretation as John carried it out, to such an extent that one cannot separate John's "biographical" interest in Paul from some imagined, distinct "exegetical" aim.

In this brief essay I shall give just a few (I hope tantalizing) selections from my "gallery exhibition" of John's portraits of his beloved Paul, and then turn specifically to the implications of this research for contemporary biblical hermeneutics, preaching, and the social imagination—the theological, historical, and exegetical payoff the Henry Luce III Fellows in Theology program both encourages and so marvelously facilitates.

Why Chrysostom Composed Verbal Portraits of Paul

A central tenet of my study is that John's exegetical art must be placed in its historical, artistic, theological, and cultural contexts. So we must begin with the question: Why did John paint verbal portraits of Paul in the first place? Not, as we might think, to preserve for posterity some memory of the exact physical details of this man, but for what John would consider higher (and no less "true") purposes. Of major importance is the fact that Paul told his readers to be "imitators of him" (1 Cor 4:16, ff.); in Greek the word for "imitator" [mimētēs] is the same as the "copyist" or "painter." (This was of course a key facet of Plato's critique of artists in book 10 of the *Republic.*) Hence John thought Paul himself asked his followers to paint self-portraits in imitation of the apostle, who was himself an imitator of Christ, and therefore "the archetype of virtue" [ho archetypos tēs aretēs], one who was the "perfect impression" of the divine seal but, unlike Christ, was fully human, and therefore thoroughly capable of imitation by other mere mortals. This fits in seamlessly with John's characteristic antique pedagogical and psychagogical assumption that one learns to act ethically by emulating virtuous exemplars.

But how can one copy the Pauline archetype without being able to put one's eyes on him? Part of the answer, for John, comes from Greek epistolary theory: a letter was said almost to "contain a portrait of the soul of its author."[13] And Paul wrote letters. So, when John interpreted those letters, he saw his task to be to uncover and display the portrait of the author inscribed therein. And here we see his love hermeneutics at work as well, for the letter was, as Cicero famously put it, *amicorum conloquia absentium,* "a conversation between absent friends."[14] The Pauline letter, which originally united friends separated by distance, now can connect those divided by death. John was further spurred to the task of Pauline portraiture by his general sense, largely derived from the fervent piety of his age, of all Scripture as comprised of "relics" of the saints of old. Hence the Pauline letters, like any other relic of the apostle (such as his shoes, his bed, the chain that bound him) provide what John seeks: direct access to the presence of the now-dead saintly author. His scriptural exposition has as its goal creating a direct and vivid encounter with the scriptural author through the placarding of vivid portrayals of him. This is how John describes the preaching task: "For here we are employed in painting portraits, royal portraits . . . Moreover, our stylus is the tongue, and the artist the Holy Spirit."[15]

The Portraits Themselves

John's literary portraits of Paul may be divided into two categories, following their graphic counterparts—miniature and full-scale
portraits. The techniques of John's Pauline portraiture are three,
all derived from the Greco-Roman rhetoric in which he was schooled:
the epithet, the encomium, and the *ekphrasis*.

a. *Miniature portraits (epithets)*

John's miniature portraits of Paul are composed in the form of
epithets. An epithet is a type of rhetorical shorthand by which a
name or an attribute of a person serves crisply and deftly to name
him or her. From a literary point of view, epithets are instances of
the rhetorical trope *antonomasia*, the substitution of either a title,
a characteristic, or an action of a person for his or her name.[16] Logi-
cally epithets, as portraits in shorthand, often work by synecdoche,
the rhetorical figure by which a whole is represented by a single
part. The most memorable and conspicuous places where epithets
were used in ancient literature and society were in the great epic
poems (all remember Homer's "stouthearted Odysseus" [Odysseos
talasiphronos] and "flashing-eyed Athena" [glaukōpis Athēnē], and
in cultic prayer and imprecations by which a divine figure is in-
voked and addressed.[17] By filling the liturgical space with names of
a deity, one conjures up that deity's presence. In his liturgical homilies John summons the famous apostle by invoking him via many
names, each of which in a word or two sends a vivid image of Paul
onto one's brain. Epithets could be stacked up for rhetorical effect,
because the orator's goal is not a fixation on *"the"* portrait of the one
he names, but rather a blizzard of redolent images to enwrap the
psyche of the hearer in contemplation of the "moving" images of a
life of faith. As one example of many such lists in John's writings,
listen to the following homiletical crescendo:

> For Paul the apostle, the vessel of election, the
> temple of God, the mouth of Christ, the lyre of the
> spirit, the teacher of the world, the one who
> circumnavigated land and sea, the one who drew
> back the thorns of sins, the one who scattered the
> seeds of piety, the one who was wealthier than kings,
> more powerful than the rich, stronger than soldiers,

> wiser than philosophers, better-spoken than
> rhetoricians, the one who though having nothing
> possessed it all, the one who could destroy death by
> his shadow, the one who sent diseases fleeing by his
> clothing, the one who stopped the winds in the sea,
> the one who was snatched up into the third heaven
> and entered into paradise, the one who proclaimed
> Christ to be God, that one says . . . .[18]

Each one of these tiny Pauline portraits encapsulates in a single word or phrase a well-known and easily recognized aspect of the apostle's career, identity, or life history. The long list serves to emphasize grandly that Paul excels all others in every conceivable arena of competition.

b. Full scale portraits (encomium and ekphrasis)

Miniature portraits trigger the memory of the hearers to recall fuller narratives and depictions that they already know. The full-scale portraits of Paul that John composes are cast in the form of the ancient encomium. One of the most stable and enduring rhetorical forms in the history of Greek literature, the encomium, or speech in praise of a subject, was constructed according to a conventional list of topics an orator could choose from in lauding his subject.[19] Customarily the proof of an encomium was divided into body, soul, and "external circumstances." All three elements were thought to make up the human life that the orator sought to recreate in the non-fleshly medium of words. John knows this division (he cites it directly at times),[20] and engaged all three topics in his lavish praises of Paul.

In painting Paul before his audience, John also employed the highly adaptable rhetorical form called *ekphrasis*: "a descriptive discourse which visibly brings the object being manifested before one's eyes,"[21] "a painting in words."[22] Some of the most famous *ekphraseis* preserved from antiquity are descriptions of works of art—paintings, statues, architecture—but a person could also be a fitting subject for an *ekphrasis*. An *ekphrasis* usually involved the retelling of an already familiar story as the backdrop to the work of art or individual being described. Consequently, it was the perfect vehicle for John's rhetorical and catechetical purpose: to orchestrate through his preaching a living encounter between Paul and his hearers which would generate the same acute emotional response he himself felt for the apostle, which, he hoped, would lead to deeper emulation of that model of virtue. John himself brings his ekphrastic art and encomiastic form together for this purpose and rhetorical effect as he directly states: "Just now when we were praising the blessed Paul you jumped for joy because you saw him present."[23]

1. Body

John overtly employed the form of *ekphrasis* in one crucial passage where he describes Paul's body by actually summoning up (via his oratory) an imaginary Pauline painting that he will then depict in such vivid terms that his audience will be transformed from auditors to spectators (the stated goal of an *ekphrasis*).

> Let's see then how Paul imitated [mimēsasthai] Christ. For this imitation [mimēsis] needs not time and art, but only the exercise of one's free will. For if we go into a painter's studio, we shall not be able to copy [mimēsasthai] the portrait [eikōn], even if we see it ten thousand times. But it is by hearing alone that we can copy him. So, do you wish us to bring the tablet into the middle here and sketch [hypographein] for you Paul's way of life? Well, let it be set before you, the picture far more illustrious than the portraits of the emperors. For what underlies it is not boards glued together, nor canvas stretched out; but the work of God is what underlies it, for it is a soul and a body. . . . Now, let's assume our tablet is Paul's soul. This tablet was not long ago lying covered with soot, full of cobwebs. (For nothing is worse than blasphemy.) But when the one who refashions everything came, and saw that it wasn't through carelessness and laziness that Paul was drawn this way, but through inexperience, and his not having the bright tincture of piety (for he had zeal, but the colors [chrōmata] were not there, because he did not have "the zeal according to knowledge" [Rom 10:2]), he gives him the bright tincture of the truth, that is, grace. And all at once he exhibited the imperial portrait [hē basilikē eikōn]. For after receiving the colors and learning the things of which he was ignorant, he did not wait for a long time, but immediately he appeared as an excellent artist [technitēs aristos]. And first he shows the imperial head, by preaching Christ. Then also he

shows the rest of the body, the body of accurate
conduct. For painters shut themselves up, and do
all their work with great accuracy and silence, not
opening the doors to anyone. But Paul, setting out
his tablet in the midst of the world, with everyone
opposing him, and causing tumult and agitation,
made this imperial portrait so, and he was not
hindered. That is why he said, "We have become a
spectacle to the world" (1 Cor 4:9). In the midst of
land and sea, of heaven and the whole earth, and of
the cosmos, things material and spiritual, he was
painting his portrait [tēn eikona zōgraphōn]. Would
you like to see the other parts of the portrait also,
from the head down? Or would you like to start from
below and move up the body?[24]

After this introduction to the *ekphrasis*, John continues with individual portraits of Paul's feet ("What could be more beautiful than
these feet . . . !"), his chest, belly, hands, and back. In the conclusion
to this long excursus, even Paul's fingernail makes a surprise appearance.[25]

2. Soul

One would think a soul harder to describe than a body, but this
poses no difficulty for John, because he regards Paul's soul as a
composite portrait made up of individual virtues, all of which, like
a palette of colors, make up the "meadow of virtues" that Paul's soul
constituted.[26] Hence in John's writings are many portraits of Paul's
soul that show him superior to all other claimants in specific virtues—love, tenderness, self-control, moderation, humility, zeal, cour-
age, endurance. Comparison is essential to the form of the encomium, for the orator offers praise for his subject by setting him
alongside other esteemed worthies and demonstrating that he or
she far outstrips them. We see this proof by comparison used by
John in one argument in which he offers an alchemical portrait of
Paul's soul, and concludes that a new "table of elements" would be
required to provide an accurate depiction of its substance:

What might one call that soul? Golden, or steely?
For it was more solid than any steel, and more
precious than gold and precious stones. It will outdo
the former material in malleability, and the latter
in costliness. To what then might one compare it?

To none of the things which exist; but if gold could become steel, and steel gold, then perhaps in some way his soul would attain its likeness from their combination. But why must I compare it with steel and gold? Place the whole world opposite his soul, and then you will see Paul's soul outweighing it in the balance.[27]

3. Life circumstances

The third category of praise in an encomium is what the rhetoricians (and John) call "external circumstances." These are what we would regard as the biographical facts of life, including birth, ancestry, native city, parents, education, trade, deeds, friendships, reputation, rule, wealth, children, and noble death. In painting his Paul, John negotiates many complicated lines of tension for his own context (for example, on Paul's ancestry as a Jew, or his rhetorical acumen despite having had only a tentmaker's education) as he seeks to placard a Paul who fits the particular catechetical and social aims he has in mind. One of the most important "deeds" in Paul's life, from John's point of view, was of course his conversion, which marks a dividing line, as John has it from Luke, between the life of Paul the vicious persecutor and Paul the dedicated missionary. He sets that scene before the eyes of his audience in the following poetic manner:

> I desire to see this big fish caught, the fish that had roiled up the entire sea, and raised countless waves against the church. I desire to see him caught, not with a fishhook, but by a word of the Lord. For just as a fisherman sitting on a high rock, holding up his rod, lets his hook down from above into the sea, thus also our Lord, who demonstrated the spiritual fishing technique, as though sitting on the high rock of the heavens, let down this call from above, like an anchor: "Saul, Saul, why are you persecuting me?" And thus he caught this big fish.[28]

In painting these word portraits of the apostle Paul's body, soul, and life, John sought to orchestrate a real and vivid encounter between the dead saint and his audiences, so that they might sculpt their own behavior to match the archetype of virtue thus represented. That is why his encomia usually end with a summons to imitation: "Therefore let us not only admire, but emulate this archetype of virtue."[29]

Six Implications of This Research for Theology, Church, and Academy

Here I shall sketch in brief some important ramifications this study in patristic hermeneutics might have for contemporary Christian theology, ministry, and living in our time. I think there are many potentially significant implications, of which I shall name six here (and I would be delighted for others to take this work in quite different directions than I myself have envisioned).

1. Exegesis and Relationship with the Author

The art of exegesis, especially though not exclusively in the case of texts that have a named author, is embedded in a relationship between author and reader that is constructed before, during, and after the act of reading. This crucial aspect of exegetical practice—that *all* Pauline and other interpreters work from an assumed mental image of the author—requires more study and overt discussion, and might actually offer some middle options to the rigid polarization of New Testament hermeneutics between "historical-critical" and "newer" methodologies. Albert Schweitzer spoke of portraits of Jesus painted in love and painted in hate, both of which he preferred to those sketched from tepid dispositions toward the subject.[30] The same is true in Pauline studies, though it is not generally discussed. The process of engagement with the author, Paul, that each Pauline interpreter lives out in her or his lifetime of reading the letters is a very complex and multi-layered one, a record of living continual conversation with a voice that speaks, whether one comes to love it, hate it, or simply lose interest in it. Each Pauline interpreter—whether motivated by love, curiosity, cautious enthusiasm, suspicion, scepticism, or downright hatred—is answerable to the question of why she or he bothers with him in the first place.

John's "love hermeneutics" itself, I would argue, presents a dual legacy. On the one hand, it captures most evocatively the genuine reading experience of some Pauline interpreters, and challenges all readers to declare their allegiance, or at least to explore the emotional and personal dynamics of their interpretive work. But, on the other hand, one cannot just unquestioningly accept at face value his claim that love is the sole exegetical requirement or virtue. How can love for the author be tested as genuine, as guaranteeing an accurate or legitimate interpretation? How and when does love for the author become a form of exegetical narcissism, especially given the predilection—so clearly exemplified by John as well—to sketch the author in one's own likeness? Most keenly, might not love for the author blind a reader to instances where one should responsibly break the mimetic cycle, rather than endlessly replicate its ethically or theologically flawed perspective? This danger is most graphically illustrated, for instance, in John's virulent anti-Judaizing—on the claim that Paul was not just his model in vilification, but his collaborator.[31] I would suggest that what we learn from John is that the temperament and attitude of the interpreter toward the author whose letters she or he is interpreting is a crucial ingredient in interpretive praxis with which scholarship must more directly attend—openly, appreciatively, and critically. This learning advances the current hermeneutical discussion, without undiscriminatingly accepting John's claim that love is the sole exegetical requirement or virtue.

2. *Constructions of the author as acts of self-construction*

The way in which a reader creates a portrait of the author depends upon the text and other sources, to be sure, but it is also to some degree a product of the interpreting self (which is itself affected by the interpretive enterprise). Just as John portrayed Paul in ways reflective of his image (as an urban "worldly ascetic"), so also the Pauls of contemporary scholarship bear the indelible marks of the twentieth century. Even when not stated overtly, scholars today, as much as John in the fourth century, battle Pauline portraits they consider distortions of the man, his message, and their own theological, ecclesial, and social commitments. While the antitypes may not be Julian, or Nero, or Plato, the most influential counter-portraits of Paul in the last thirty years have been those of Augustine and Luther, harmonized into a single image: Paul the agonized Jew who sought to find a gracious God by means other than his own Jewish "legalistic" ethical perfectionism. Modern scholars such as E.P. Sanders and Krister Stendahl have sought to peel off the Lutheran overlay on the Pauline portrait and "restore the original" that lay behind, in his own native and distinct form.[32] That "original" has been restored by the cleaning and repainting of master artists who have done their homework, as all restorers must, in the history and conventions of the period. His anti-Semitism (the modern virus) and individualism scrubbed away, the Paul of Sanders and Stendahl has had new contours drawn in with the aid of the Dead Sea Scrolls and less biased pictures of first century Judaism seen "in its own light" and not in the refracted counterpose of an imagined, pristine, and reformative infant Christianity. These Pauline portraits are intentionally drawn with an eye on a studio model, a reconstructed mannequin of a "normal" first century Jew. For Sanders this illuminates the extent to which Paul ultimately diverges from the normative into a distinctive religious system, a portrait which must hang in a new gallery. The Paul of James D.G. Dunn is based upon the portrait refashioned by Sanders, but insists on its rightful place in the Judaica museum.[33] This version of the apostle is at home among the "old masters" of first century "covenantal Judaism,"[34] but is displayed in a discrete wing of the Judaica museum set aside for an artistic movement that challenges the establishment, in an architectural addition *meant* to be an integral part of the existing edifice (though the plumbing and electrical systems, as is so often the case, sadly never did fully coordinate). All these portraits are situated in a museum haunted by a face that doesn't deserve a picture, but nonetheless dominates the scene and the viewing experience totally: Adolf Hitler. His image—either the Chaplinesque clowning Hitler, the goosestep and salute-inspiring orator, or the Auschwitz-designing madman—explains the prevailing tendencies of fresh Pauline portraits in the second half of this century to cast Paul in deliberate antitype to Hitler and his genocidal anti-Judaism with which Christianity, with Paul as its precursor, might be deemed in collusion. The "new perspective"[35] (interestingly, an artistic term in itself) on Paul that has emerged in these last three decades, painted particularly in colors from Rom 9-11, is of a solitary religious genius with Jewish facial features who stands against Hitler, raging and sometimes weeping at the heinous uses to which his "false" evil anti-Judaistic portrayal has been put.

To cite a second, less horrific example, it is not surprising that it was in the era of "practical theology" that Paul was discovered to have been not a systematic but an occasional theologian, a pastoral thinker. But John's example also shows that there is more to this than just seeing ourselves in a mirror; John painted a gallery of

Pauline portraits out of existing sources (not just capriciously), se-
lectively appropriated them and, most importantly, was himself
changing even as his Paul was (the dead are not fixed, it seems, but
grow with us). Hence both the portrait-subject and portraitist are
locked in a dynamic dance of creative proportions. But toward what
end?

3. *Exegesis as social creation*

John employed his Pauline portraits to advocate and indeed
create a new social form—a Christian *polis*. His Paul was the "archetype of virtue" who exemplified the very qualities John thought
essential to the construction of Christian society, especially the car-
dinal virtues (justice, bravery, moderation, and prudence, along with
love and humility), and the monastic disciplines of chastity,
almsgiving, compunction and fasting. John's example—the quest
to transform late antique society by means of a portrait of Paul the
urban ascetic ethical archetype—offers a vision of the exegetical
task that will impress some contemporary readers as a dizzyingly
hopeful specter of the power of Christian discourse to transform the
world, even as it will strike others as a frightening portent of Christian compulsion to conformity inimicable to an age of religious pluralism, especially in its insistence that *all* imitate the one model.[36]
Hence Pauline portraits ultimately bring us face to face with *the*
theological and ministerial question of our day: how faithful Christian living and preaching act and interact in a climate of pluralist
ecumenical cooperation and mutual respect. Of course, Paul was
himself aware of the dilemma, though he did not solve it. He has
left it as an enigmatic legacy to his readers that they are to imitate
one who was "all things to all people" (1 Cor 9:22), a man of 1,000
faces.

4. *Exegetical products as rhetorical forms*

All exegetical work participates in literary and rhetorical conventions (even when flaunting them), is packaged in some way, and
is meant to move an audience in some direction. We have seen this
in John's use of the forms of the epithet, the encomium, and the
ekphrasis—conventional oratorical genres and techniques of his time.
John's homilies on Paul, consequently, cannot and should not be
read as though they are scholastic commentaries on Scripture. They

are homiletical expositions of the text that have quite specific catechetical, liturgical and rhetorical goals and functions. While John's expositions of Paul and his letters may be somewhat extreme instances of this rhetorical quality of exegetical practice, they are not uniquely so. Even today, all exegetical productions have a rhetoric, a persuasive strategy (does an audience that has ever heard of HarperCollins and the Historical Jesus really need to be reminded of this?), which may range from—"I want you to be interested in this as I am," to "I want you to view Jesus/Paul/the church/Christian theology/ethics the way I do." But in an age of deliberate genre-bending all around us, as fiction and biography merge in *Duke,* as television shows offer fake news broadcasts with simulations of real events, both producers and consumers of biblical interpretation need to attend to the packaging and purposes of these works. I regard this as both an opportunity and a challenge: an opportunity to harness considerable persuasive power for good ends, yet a challenge to maintain scholarly and theological integrity in the midst of mediagenic frenzy. A nice example of this fault line is provided by John's anguished ambivalence when his audiences applauded his homilies.[37] His distress is due to the fact that, on the one hand, applause is precisely what the accomplished orator seeks, but, on the other, he avers that his true goal is the transformation of lives in ethical conduct, not mere momentary adulation of his rhetorical prowess. To walk this tightrope effectively we might ask: What would it mean for contemporary biblical scholarship to think of itself as an ethical art form within this culture?

5. *Biblical Preaching as Ekphrasis*

Contemporary biblical homiletics is enriched, I think, by the notion of *ekphrasis*—a vivid description based on a narrative shared by author and audience, which seeks to make the hearer a spectator. It therefore links also with my first point, in that the preacher seeks to foster a relationship between her or his audience and the figure depicted. I also find the concept of synesthesia that lies at the heart of *ekphrasis* (i.e., working across the senses from hearing to seeing) redolent for homiletics and worship (I believe others have written on this, but perhaps John offers a nice example of it in practice that might usefully be further explored). The other implication of *ekphrasis* that I find most suggestive is the debate among art historians over whether or not the *ekphrasis* is meant to *stand along-side* the subject it describes, or, as one scholar puts it, the *ekphrasis* winds up *competing with* or *replacing* the original subject.[38] This is a suggestive way to pose the place of biblical homiletics and commentaries in relation to the text itself (a reality anyone who has taught an "Introduction to the New Testament" course knows acutely well, since the textbook always commands the students' attention at the expense of the primary text). For example, I wonder sometimes, as I read John's homilies, and revel in his sweet Greek syntax and rhetorical figures, if and how the biblical text may have been dwarfed liturgically by his sermon, even as the homily allowed John to bring Christian discourse up to a level of high culture. How do modern preachers address this dilemma, and how might John's example provide a useful framework for posing some important questions about media, worship, and the nature of canon and commentary?

Yet another element of John's art that illustrates the preaching task is the way his relationship with Paul and his letters has both a private and a public dimension, neatly symbolizing the difficult and mandatory homiletical move from study to pulpit. This reality comes to lovely graphic expression in the transformation of the iconographical type we discussed above. In a twelfth-century illustrated manuscript of John's homilies on the Pauline letters, which is housed in the Ambrosian Library in Milan, the scene looks at once familiar from the inspired author portrait, but a significant shift has taken place.[39] The slanted writing surface before which John stands, with Paul hovering over his shoulder, has become a pulpit, upon which John's homily hangs, and as it dips over the front of the lectern, the sermon scroll becomes a font of water from which a host of clergy and the faithful eagerly drink. Proclos is still there, but, since it is no longer a private picture, he has come out of hiding to be a suppliant reacting to the grandeur of what he, along with the others, sees. And the artist added one more, highly significant element: Christ himself from heaven sends down his own spray of inspiration to John's hand, thus theologically expanding the horizon of the one-on-one encounter between author and reader. The juxtaposition of the two scenes in the iconography of one of the most famous of all Christian preachers illustrates an ineluctable dynamic lived by preachers every week: the movement from solitary work at a desk to face-to-face encounters with crowds of listeners, from private study to public exposition and exhortation. The preacher's difficult task is effectively to bridge the spaces of silence and of speech, so that each rightly informs the other.

6. *Life as self-portraiture*

John painted his verbal portraits of Paul because he believed the Christian life is a quest for the most accurate self-portrait of Christ. Because in post-Nicene theology Christ's divinity was so highly elevated that people in the pews could rightly complain that they should hardly be expected to emulate him, John found in Paul a mortal, fully terrestrial exemplar he could urge on his congregants: "for as I have repeatedly said, and shall not stop saying, 'the same body was in him as is in us, the same rearing, and the same soul.'"[40] This concept of life as ethical self-sculpting may perhaps be profitably retrieved in a contemporary American society that contests in the market arena issues of the freedom and limits of "self-creation" (body building, body carving, plastic surgery, "designer genes"). The rhetoric of denunciation of these practices often gives the impression that the project of self-creation is a modern oddity, a new-age permutation caused by space-age technologies. But it would surely be useful to engage these discussions with a sense of historical perspective and of the frank linkages that exist with the Christian ascetic project of bodily control and self-fashioning, of which John is a prime exponent. And the contemporary discussion would be enriched by an insistence upon equal attention to the sculpting of the ethical self alongside the body beautiful. But that conversation also entails the larger questions of what are the archetypes contemporary persons and religious communities seek to offer their children and themselves as objects for imitation, and how are those archetypes, like John's Paul, themselves created and disseminated?

In one of the most remarkable reversals of religious ideology imaginable, John in the late fourth century called upon his congregational audiences to strive to become "imperial portraits" [eikones basilikai], in imitation of Paul (who had imitated Christ, who was the very eikōn of God, according to 2 Cor 4:4). This is shocking when we remember that in the first three centuries imperial images—portraits, standards, or medallions that honored Roman emperors, dead and (increasingly) even living, as divine entities—constituted the fault line for Christian participation in the *imperium Romanum*. Indeed, imperial portraits were used as an instrument of local persecution of Christians, who were forced either to swear an oath or offer a small sacrificial gesture of libation or incense to show their allegiance to the gods of state, or be executed. Pliny the Younger's famous exchange of letters with the emperor Trajan gives the Roman point of view;[41] the Book of Revelation, even if not contemporary with Pliny, in its repudiation of "the image of the beast" [hē eikōn tou thēriou], reveals the early Christian perspective on such "imperial portraits" [eikones basilikai].[42] But by John's time the emperor was himself a Christian, and "imperial portraits" meant not idolatrous images, but rather the highest artistic standards employed for the divinely approved sovereign. And, by a neat wordplay, the imperial or royal portraits [basilikai] could refer, not just to those of the emperor, but those of "the King," which in a Christian context referred with ease to God, in whose image all humanity was created. Hence the Christian life itself could be summed up as the quest to paint one's own self-portrait in the *imago Dei,* in imitation of Paul, in imitation of Christ. Now the image of the beast-become-beauty was to be the object of pursuit—and not only in cultic practice, but in personal piety. Paul's "sidewalk art of the soul" became for John the very model of his instructions to catechumens: to work on the charcoal sketch of their souls before baptism, at which point the permanent colors would be melted into place, to form an indelible impression of the self.

> Consider the soul to be your portrait [eikōn]. So, before the true tempera of the spirit comes, wipe away the habits which have been wrongly put into it [a long list of sins follows] . . . correct your habits, so that when the colors are laid upon it, and the imperial portrait [he basilike eikōn] shines forth, no longer will you wipe things out again, and damage or scar the beauty which has been given to you by God.[43]

This vision of the Christian moral life as an artistic project has been given multiform expression in the history of Christian thought, but perhaps nowhere as brilliantly as in the constellations of words and images created by William Blake. In "The Laocoön," an illuminated printing on a plate featuring an image of God and his two sons—Adam and Satan—amongst a whirl of reflections we find the following meditation:

> Prayer is the Study of Art
> Praise is the Practice of Art
> Fasting &c. all relate to Art . . .

> Practice is Art   If you leave off you are Lost

> A Poet a Painter a Musician an Architect: the Man
> Or Woman who is not one of these is not a Christian
> You must leave Fathers & Mothers & Houses and
> Lands
> if they stand in the way of Art[44]

Endnotes

1.   The present essay is derived from my book, *The Heavenly Trumpet: John Chrysostom and the Art of Pauline Interpretation* (Hermeneutische Untersuchungen zur Theologie 40; Tübingen: J. C. B. Mohr [Paul Siebeck] 2000; Louisville: Westminster/John Knox, 2002, forthcoming), which was completed during my year as a Luce Fellow (used here with permission of the publishers). This abbreviated version was originally a presentation to the Henry Luce III Fellows in Theology Conference in October 1999; another version of it was presented as the Alexander Thompson Lecture at Princeton Theological Seminary, in March 2000. I would like to thank Professor Wayne A. Meeks for his most insightful response on the former occassion.

2.   *hom. in Rom.* Argumentum 1 [J.-P. Migne, *Patrologia Cursus Completus. Series Graeca* (hereafter, *PG*) 60.391].

3.   See Peter Brown, *The Cult of the Saints: Its Rise and Function in Latin Christianity* (Haskell Lectures on the History of Religions, new series no. 2; Chicago: University of Chicago Press, 1981), 50.

4.   *hom. in 2 Cor. 11:1* 1 [*PG* 51.301], my translation (as with all quotations from Chrysostom's writings in this essay). The abbreviated titles for Chrysostom's writings follow Geoffrey William Hugo Lampe, *A Patristic Greek Lexicon* (Oxford: Clarendon Press, 1961), xvii-iii.

5.   Photograph by Leonidas Ananiades, used with permission of the National Library, Athens.

6.   George of Alexandria, *vita Joh. Chrys.* 27 (text from François Halkin, *Douze récits byzantins sur Saint Jean Chrysostome* [Subsidia hagiographica 60; Brussels: Société des Bollandistes, 1977], 142-48).

7.   *Epistulae* 5.32 (to Isidore the Deacon) [*PG* 78.1348].

8.   In *hom. in 2 Tim.* 9.2 [*PG* 62.652], Chrysostom describes the physical act of reading as "taking the apostle in hand" [ton apostolon meta cheiras labōn], and "examining" [periskepsamenos] a given passage. Here "the apostle" is used as a metonym for the codex of his letters, an ancient coalescence of author and text that was al-

ready used in the New Testament in reference to the Pentateuch (Moses) and the Psalms (David) (see Lk 16:29; 24:27; Heb 4:7). The same idea is expressed, even more poetically, in *hom. in 2 Cor.* 21.4 [*PG* 61.546]: "let us continually have him in our hands, delighting in his writings as in a meadow and garden." Here Chrysostom makes a deliberate word play with metacheirizesthai, which means both to take in hand, and to pursue, as in learning or philosophy (Liddell-Scott-Jones, *Greek-English Lexicon* [Oxford: Clarendon, 1968], 1118).

9.   *hom. in Rom.* Argumentum 1 [*PG* 60.391].

10.   Here I am building upon the important thesis of Peter Brown, that Chrysostom was engaged in an effort to reconstitute the *polis* of Antioch: "John elevated the Christian household so as to eclipse the ancient city. He refused to see Antioch as a traditional civic community, bound together by a common civic patriotism, expressed by shared rhythms of collective festivity. He made no secret of the fact that he wished the theater, the hippodrome, even the busy agora, to fall silent forever. The Antioch of his dearest hopes was to be no more than a conglomeration of believing households, joined by a common meeting-place within the spacious courtyards of the Great Church. He wished the doors of the Christian house to swing to, shutting out the murmur of a late classical metropolis" (Peter Brown, *The Body and Society: Men, Women, and Sexual Renunciation in Early Christianity* [Lectures in the History of Religions, new series no. 13; New York: Columbia University Press, 1988], 313). What I wish to add to Brown's argument is an analysis of the important role of the apostle Paul in this overarching project, whom Chrysostom uses as the exemplar of the kind of lay monastic piety he seeks to foster among his congregants.

11.   *hom. in Rom. 16:3* 1.1 [*PG* 51.187-88].

12.   To borrow a phrase from the title of Vincent L. Wimbush's book on 1 Corinthians 7 (*Paul the Worldly Ascetic: Response to the World and Self-Understanding According to 1 Corinthians 7* [Macon: Mercer University Press, 1987]).

13.   Pseudo-Demetrius, *de elocutione* 4.227.

14.   Cicero, *Philippics* 2.4.

15.   *hom. in Ac.* 30.4 [*PG* 60.227-28].

16.   Quintilian, *Institutio Oratoria* 8.6.29: "Antonomasia, which substitutes something else for a proper name [*quae aliquid pro nomine ponit*], is very common in poets: it may be done in two ways: by the substitution of an epithet as equivalent to the name which it replaces [*et per epitheton, quod detracto eo, cui apponitur, valet pro nomine*], such as 'Tydides' [=son of Tydeus], 'Pelides' [=son of Peleus, Achilles], or by indicating the most striking characteristics of an individual [*et ex his, quae in quoque sunt praecipua*], as in the phrase 'Father of gods and king of men,' or from acts clearly indicating the individual [*et ex factis, quibus persona signatur*], as in the phrase, 'The arms which he, the traitor, left fixed on the chamber wall.'"

17.   For an entry into the considerable research that has been done into epithets for the Greek gods and heroes, see H. J. Rose (updated by Simon Hornblower), "Epithets, Divine," *The Oxford Classical Dictionary*, ed. Simon Hornblower and Anthony Spawforth (3rd. ed.; Oxford: Oxford University Press, 1996), 401-402; and Paolo Vivante, *The Epithets in Homer: A Study in Poetic Values* (New Haven: Yale University Press, 1982).

18.   *de Lazaro* 6.9 [*PG* 48.1041].

19.   For an introduction to the encomium and its sources see Theodore C. Burgess, *Epideictic Literature* (The University of Chicago Studies in Classical Philology; Chicago: University of Chicago Press, 1902); *Menander Rhetor*, edited with translation and commentary by D. A. Russell and N. G. Wilson (Oxford: Clarendon Press, 1981), "Introduction: Epideictic Practice and Theory," xi-xxxiv; George A. Kennedy, *Greek Rhetoric Under Christian Emperors* (Princeton: Princeton University Press, 1983),

23-27, 52-132; Margaret M. Mitchell, *Paul and the Rhetoric of Reconciliation: An Exegetical Investigation of the Language and Composition of 1 Corinthians* (Hermeneutische Untersuchungen zur Theologie 28; Tübingen: J. C. B. Mohr [Paul Siebeck], 1991; Louisville: Westminster/John Knox, 1993), 213-21; still valuable is Richard Volkmann, *Die Rhetorik der Griechen und Römer in systematischer Übersicht* (repr. ed.; Hildesheim: Georg Olms, 1987 [original Leipzig: Teubner, 1885]), 314-61.

20. *hom. in 1 Tim.* 1.1 [*PG* 62.505]; *laud. Paul.* 4.21 [*Sources chrétiennes* (hereafter, *SC*) 300.228]; cf. *hom. in 2 Cor.* 24.2 [*PG* 61.565]; *oppugn.* 2.5 [*PG* 47.339-40].

21. This quotation is from the second century C.E. rhetorician Theon, in his book of rhetorical exercises, *Progymnasmata* §11 (text in Leonard von Spengel, *Rhetores Graeci* [3 vols.; Leipzig: Teubner, 1853-56] 2.118).

22. See Thomas E. Ameringer, *The Stylistic Influence of the Second Sophistic on the Panegyrical Sermons of St. John Chrysostom: A Study in Greek Rhetoric* (Ph.D. diss.; Catholic University of America, 1921), 86; also Glanville Downey, "Ekphrasis," *Reallexikon für Antike und Christentum* 5 (1959): 921-44; Henry Maguire, *Art and Eloquence in Byzantium* (Princeton: Princeton University Press, 1981), 22-52; Liz James and Ruth Webb, "To Understand Ultimate Things and Enter Secret Places: Ekphrasis and Art in Byzantium," *Art History* 14 (1991): 1-17; Jás Elsner, *Art and the Roman Viewer: The Transformation of Art from the Pagan World to Christianity* (Cambridge: Cambridge University Press, 1995), 21-39.

23. *kal.* 1 [*PG* 48.953].

24. *hom. in 1 Cor.* 13.3 [*PG* 61.110-11].

25. *hom. in 1 Cor.* 13.4 [*PG* 61.112].

26. *laud. Paul.* 1.1 [SC 300.112].

27. *laud. Paul.* 2.7 [SC 300.154].

28. *hom. in Ac. 9:1* 1.3 [*PG* 51.117].

29. *laud. Paul.* 2.10 [*SC* 300.158].

30. "But it was not only each epoch that found its reflection in Jesus; each individual created Him in accordance with his own character. There is no historical task which so reveals a man's true self as the writing of a Life of Jesus. No vital force comes into the figure unless a man breathes into it all the hate or all the love of which he is capable. The stronger the love, or the stronger the hate, the more life-like is the figure which is produced" (Albert Schweitzer, *The Quest of the Historical Jesus: A Critical Study of Its Progress from Reimarus to Wrede* [New York: MacMillan, 1968, original 1906], 4).

31. *Jud.* 2.3; 3.3; 6.1 [*PG* 48.862, 864, 903].

32. Krister Stendahl, "The Apostle Paul and the Introspective Conscience of the West," *Harvard Theological Review* 56 (1963): 199-215, reprinted idem, *Paul Among Jews and Gentiles and Other Essays* (Philadelphia: Fortress Press, 1976), 78-96; E.P. Sanders, *Paul and Palestinian Judaism: A Comparison of Patterns of Religion* (Philadelphia: Fortress Press, 1977); idem, *Paul, the Law, and the Jewish People* (Philadelphia: Fortress Press, 1983).

33. Among James D.G. Dunn's many publications on Paul, see especially the essays in *Jesus, Paul and the Law: Studies in Mark and Galatians* (Louisville: Westminster/John Knox Press, 1990); *The Theology of Paul's Letter to the Galatians* (Cambridge: Cambridge University Press, 1993); *The Theology of Paul the Apostle* (Grand Rapids: W.B. Eerdmans, 1998).

34. Portraits of Paul emphasizing his Jewishness of course have a long history (see the brief summary in Sanders, *Paul and Palestinian Judaism*, 1-12). The most im-

portant recent depictions of Paul by Jewish scholar-portraitists have accented his ultimate divergence from Judaism: Alan F. Segal, *Paul the Convert: The Apostolate and Apostasy of Saul the Pharisee* (New Haven/London: Yale University Press, 1990), who organizes his study around three "portraits": Paul the Jew, Paul the Convert, and Paul the Apostle; and Daniel Boyarin, *A Radical Jew: Paul and the Politics of Identity* (Berkeley: University of California Press, 1994), who largely sides with Dunn (see 51-56). And then, of course, there is the revival of the old (melo)dramatic picture of Paul as not really a Jew, but a scheming proselyte, by Hyam Maccoby, *The Mythmaker: Paul and the Invention of Christianity* (San Francisco: Harper & Row, 1986).

35. The phrase was coined by Dunn (James D.G. Dunn, "The New Perspective on Paul," *Bulletin of the John Rylands University Library of Manchester* 65 [1983]: 95-122, repr. with an additional note in idem, *Jesus, Paul and the Law*, 183-214).

36. See the concerns expressed by Elizabeth A. Castelli, *Imitating Paul: A Discourse of Power* (Literary Currents in Biblical Interpretation; Louisville: Westminster/John Knox, 1991), especially 119-36.

37. See, for example, *Jud.* 1.1 [*PG* 48.814]; *Laz.* 2.3; 7.1 [*PG* 48.985, 1045].

38. Elsner, *Art and the Roman Viewer*, 27.

39. The image is *Milan, Ambrosian A 172, Sup.*, fol. 263^V, plate 4 in Mitchell, *Heavenly Trumpet*; a full discussion, bibliography, and five more plates of iconographical images of Chrysostom and Paul may be found in Appendix 2 of my book, 488-99.

40. *laud. Paul.* 4.21 [*SC* 300.228].

41. See Pliny, *Ep.* 10.96.5-6.

42. Rev 13:14-15; 14:9, 11; 15:2; 16:2; 19:20; 20:4; cf. Mk 12:16f.

43. *catech.* 2.3 [49.235]. Here Chrysostom balances the paraenetical paradox of the indicative and the imperative ("you are the image of God"/ "become the image of God"), by urging his converts to be good portraits who do not deface the divine image they bear.

44. William Blake, "The Laocoön," *The Complete Poetry and Prose of William Blake*, ed. David V. Erdman, commentary by Harold Bloom (rev. ed.; New York: Doubleday, 1988), 274 (text), 272 (plate). I would like to thank Prof. Jennifer Jesse of Truman State University for pointing me to this remarkable composition.

Song of Songs: Ecumenical Christianities as Earth Faiths

Larry Rasmussen
UNION THEOLOGICAL SEMINARY
NEW YORK, NEW YORK

"Song of Songs" is a double reference. The earthy little book of the Hebrew Bible is the obvious one. Its dual love story—sensuous love between human beings, as voiced by a woman, a man, and a group of women, and the sensuous love of these passionate souls for the land and its life—serves as a backdrop to these pages. The other reference is not as obvious. But it is more direct. It is a statement of Dietrich Bonhoeffer in a 1928 address on "the foundations of Christian ethics." Bonhoeffer says: "The earth remains our mother, just as God remains our Father, and our mother will only lay in the Father's arms those who remain true to her. Earth and its distress—that is the Christian's Song of Songs."[1]

The goal of this Luce project as a whole is to offer Christian spiritual-moral frames and practices that address social and ecological issues together (Earth's "distress") and that do so in ways that contribute to a religiously rooted Earth ethic. Three components are entailed. One is reconstructed Christian moral theory that encompasses socio-communal, biophysical, and geoplanetary dynamics. The whole Community of Life has moral standing. A second is a presentation of the traditions and practices of Christian "Earth faiths." These are Christianities, past and present, whose fidelity to God is or was measured by a certain criterion: their contribution to Earth's care and redemption. The third component is a presentation of Christian contributions to sustainable, Earth-enhancing ways of living, within ecclesial structures and beyond them.

The chief means for this work will be a book in Christianity and culture, coupled with a CD-ROM and/or a website that utilizes the book's content as well as supplementary materials. Both the book and CD-ROM/website will present the "deep traditions" of Earth-oriented Christianities as expressed in past and present communities and their practices, together with extensive theo-ethical explication. The book, CD-ROM and/or website will all use visuals as well as text. Most of the visuals and some of the text will be supplied by the communities visited.

Key assumptions inform this research. Some involve methodological judgments, some are historical, theological, and ecclesiological convictions. No effort is made to sort them here, but simply to display them.

1. Until matters of "eco-justice" are seen to rest somewhere near the heart of Christian faith, "the environment" will be relegated to the long list of important but disparate "issues" clamoring for people's attention. This research project argues that the proper subject of justice itself is not "the environment" or even "society," but inclusive "creation" (the more-than-human and human, together). It argues further that all creation has standing before God and is the object of redemption. Creation's well-being rests at the center, not the edge, of Christian moral responsibility and practices, liturgical and contemplative practices included. So the terms for adequate moral theory are an inclusive sense of creation and an inclusive notion of justice.

2. A significant work for Christian communities for the foreseeable future is adapting their major teachings and practices—what this study will call the "deep traditions" of Christianity—to the task of revaluing nature/culture together so as to prevent their destruction and contribute to their sustainability.

3. There are no pristine Christian traditions for this task. "Conversions to Earth" are crucial to Christianity's part in the shared interreligious and pan-human vocation of Earthkeeping. "Conversion" here means what it has commonly meant in religious experience; namely, both a break with the past and yet a preservation of essential trajectories; both a rupture and new direction, yet a sense that the new place is also "home" or truly "home"; both a rejection of elements of tradition yet the making of new tradition in fulfillment of the old; both difference from what has gone before and solidarity with it. Substantively, "conversion to Earth" means measuring all Christian impulses by their contribution to Earth's well-being.

4. Valorizing Christian pluralism is both necessary and desirable. It is necessary for the sake of the integrity of diverse Christian traditions themselves. They are many; they are often wildly different from one another; and they ought to be treated in ways that honor their genealogy and merit the respect and recognition of

their devotees. This project assumes that the church's catholicity itself is a name for the community of churches around the world that manifest the ecumenical range of historically incarnate faiths lived across two millennia on most of the Earth's continents. Such catholicity is inherently plural and can only exist as internally diverse. A faithful remembering of the Christian past means retrieving this variety in so far as possible. This is not faithfulness in the manner of imperial Christianities large and small, which consists, in part, in the selective forgetting or repression of this variety (usually in the name of theological heresy, moral deviance, or simply cultural prejudice). Rather, this is faithfulness as multiple Christianities on most of the continents and as evidenced from the most formative years themselves, beginning in the Jewish renewal movements of the first century C.E. and spreading quickly through the multi-cultural, multi-linguistic, multi-racial, and multi-ethnic plurality of peoples and places on the three continents surrounding the Mediterranean Basin.

5. Valorizing Christian pluralism is desirable for another reason. The "eco-crisis" is comprehensive of nature and culture together. No one tradition, religious or secular, can satisfactorily address the full range of matters that require planetary attention. It is necessary to think ecologically about ecumenism and ecumenically about ecological well-being.

6. Retrieving and sometimes transforming the deep traditions of Christianity means, for valorized Christian pluralism, that "traditioning" entails living with two or more truths at once, with differences of history, culture, and ways of life understood and argued as faithfully Christian. It means that revelation relates to diversity in a more complex way than the formulations of orthodoxy vs. heresy and heterodoxy, or truth vs. error, usually reflect. Revelation and diversity are related in a way akin to Aquinas's argument that God did not create one species only, because the fullness of revelation requires a fullness of means.

7. The revelation of God and God's ways are not limited to those known by and lived in the Christian churches. The argument itself can be and has been made on Christian grounds: Just as the God Israel worships is not the God of the Jews alone, by their own confession, so the God of Christians is not the God of Christians alone, by their own confession. This means that my reading of Chris-

tian traditions for this project has more to do "with a Christian reading of the past than it does with an exclusive reading of the Christian past."[2]

8. The investigation of plural Christian traditions will center in community practices and distinct ways of life. This assumes two things relevant to ethics. It assumes that the way a community "*does* the truth"—its practices—reflects its operative understandings together with its hopes or aspirations. And it assumes that the community's moral values and beliefs cannot be separated from other beliefs and prizings. How community members understand their lives comprehensively, and enact them in their practices, already entails norms for their conduct and exhibits their sense of moral responsibility as a whole. Morality is not a sector in life; it is a dimension of life intimately related to other dimensions.

9. Against the reigning assumption that Christianity is a text-based and not a place-based religion, this study assumes there are always meaningful connections of spirituality and practice to place, to environs, often to the natural landscape itself. (Desert and mountain spirituality largely mirror "the solace of fierce landscapes,"[3] for example.) This study's investigation of communities will therefore include a description of flora and geology as well as the built environment, precisely as spiritually and morally significant. The connection of locality and the spiritual-moral universe, however, is not a connection made in the manner of the tourist or the scientist. It is the landscape (to note one example) as alive among those who live their lives in a given place, the landscape as seen in reigning metaphors and symbols, in diet and dress, art and architecture, in liturgy, hymnody, prayer and preaching, in the designation of "special" or "sacred" places, and in the tasks and meaning of everyday work. At the same time, this research assumes that a sense of place and roots has been lost by some Christian peoples and that this is a casualty of modernity (the upending of settled community is one of the consistent themes of recent centuries). So the question of a "rooted" Christianity in a dynamic world is a question pursued throughout the study, both for those who continue to exhibit it and for those who do not.

10. The descriptive account of each community's place and the presence of that in the community's life—its "eco-location"—is only

part of the analysis, however. The method of analysis for this project includes other elements:

- interstructured moral analysis (socio-eco-location seen in race, gender, class, culture, and geography);
- reflection and theory as emergent from the practices and ways of life described, using interdisciplinary methods;
- analysis that is theologically as well as morally explicit;
- analysis that can be ably communicated to the churches and communities it serves;
- proposals that aim at community spiritual-moral formation and public policy;
- a working style that is itself collaborative from onset to conclusion;
- work that reconstructs Christian moral theory itself and clarifies the nature and contributions of plural Christianities as "earth faiths."

11. This project assumes that community and social justice is a strong and enduring vocational emphasis of the "peoples of the Book"—Judaism, Islam, Christianity. Divine power is experienced as the power to create a people whose way of life is to exemplify righteousness and moral responsibility.[4]

12. This project's specific theo-moral point of departure draws from liberation theologies in that it seeks out Christian communities and traditions whose opposition to experienced and perceived injustice are crucial sources of knowledge and participation for Christian revaluing of nature/culture and for the construction of just and sustainable communities. Differently said, engaging Christian communities that have suffered more than benefited from the forces of modernity is the path this research takes. This is the case in part because the forces of modernity have largely created the present threats to life. Those who have known firsthand the destructive side of modernity offer critical knowledge largely neglected by or hidden to those who have benefited.

13. The forces of modernity can be described in many ways. Describing them is essential to the work here. The crucial nexus chosen is the interaction of the global economy and global life systems. The means of treating this is by way of three successive waves of "globalization:"[5] conquest and colonization, with Christianity and commerce moving outward from Europe beginning in the fifteenth

century and understood as the spread of "civilization"; post-Second World War "development" and its economic criterion for social well-being; namely, that the well-being of all peoples is to be judged on the basis of rising production and consumption enabled by unending economic growth; and post-1989 free trade capitalism and its use of market logic, relationships, and values as the model for society itself. The old Western mission of '*mission civilisatrice*' is reaffirmed by each wave, sometimes in religious and sometimes in secular form but always to the transformation of local nature/culture and often to their destruction.

14. It is assumed, at least as a starting point, that the deep traditions and practices of the Christian communities visited may harbor local knowledge important for building just and sustainable local communities. This includes the ways of "traditional ecologists," persons whose knowledge of local and regional life-systems can undergird potentially sustainable practices. Generally speaking, premodern religions are comprehensive healing systems that include important local arts. Often these are arts for the healing of the land, arts that have, together with their practitioners, been largely disdained and shunted aside by modernity's industrialized ways, industrialized agriculture and mining included.

15. This research assumes that a scheme of inquiry and interpretation that begins in suspicion of current arrangements can, through the uncovering of subjugated pasts, move beyond retrieval of neglected memories and practices to positive construction of an Earth ethic together, provided the table is set for a dialogue of equals. It also assumes that setting the table in this way requires great labor and is far more difficult than current talk of "celebrating differences" and "embracing diversity" in the interests of "community" lets on. Granting subjugated knowledges equal voice means granting subjugated peoples equal voice. And this means power-sharing rather than "celebrating differences."

With these assumptions governing the research, the project falls into three distinct parts, as described below.

Part I "Give Us Word of the Humankind We Left to Thee"

There is an extraordinary passage in the 1907 volume that helped launch the Social Gospel movement. It is Walter

Rauschenbusch's portrayal of the gathering of the spirits of centuries past. "When the Nineteenth Century died," Rauschenbusch writes, "its Spirit descended to the vaulted chamber of the Past, where the Spirits of the dead Centuries sit on granite thrones together."[6] There the Spirit of the Eighteenth Century asked for the mandated report: "Tell thy tale, brother. Give us word of the humankind we left to thee."[7] What follows, as the witness of the Nineteenth Century, is only plausible as an expression of the extraordinary belief in Western-style progress that Rauschenbusch and his generation breathed daily.

> I am the Spirit of the Wonderful Century. I gave men mastery over nature. Discoveries and inventions, which lighted the black space of the past like lovely stars, have clustered in the Milky Way of radiance under my rule. One man does by the touch of his hand what the toil of a thousand slaves never did. Knowledge has unlocked the mines of wealth, and the hoarded wealth of today creates the vaster wealth of tomorrow. Man has escaped the slavery of Necessity and is free.

> I freed the thoughts of men. They face the facts and know their knowledge is common to all. The deeds of the East at even are known in the West at morn. They send their whispers under the seas and across the clouds.

> I broke the chains of bigotry and despotism. I made men free and equal. Every man feels the worth of his manhood.

> I have touched the summit of history. I did for mankind what none of you did before. They are rich. They are wise. They are free.[8]

In Rauschenbusch's report the Spirits of the dead Centuries sit in silence for awhile, "with troubled eyes." Eventually the Spirit of the First Century speaks and asks a series of questions about the claims of the Nineteenth Century that "You have made men rich . . .You have made men wise . . . You have set them free . . . You have made them one."[9] The Spirit of the Nineteenth Century listens carefully, its head sinks to its breast, and it says:

> Your shame is already upon me. My great cities are as yours were. My millions live from hand to mouth.

> Those who toil longest have the least. My thousands
> sink exhausted before their days are half spent. My
> human wreckage multiplies. Class faces class in
> sullen distrust. Their freedom and knowledge has
> only made men keener to suffer.[10]

Pensive, and now with troubled eyes of its own, the Spirit of the Nineteenth Century can only issue a request: "Give me a seat among you, and let me think why it has been so."[11]

Rauschenbusch wrote that as the Twentieth Century was born. It is left to us to imagine what the Spirit of the Twentieth Century had to say as this century came to a close, and what searing questions have yet to be asked in response. We, too, will have to "think why it has been so."

Of course, the extraordinary fact may well be a simple one. Perhaps both the tally of unprecedented accomplishment and the litany of shame that Rauschenbusch penned could simply be repeated. After all, the Twentieth Century both promised more than the Nineteenth and delivered on it. Goods and services increased fiftyfold. Lifetimes for millions, even billions, doubled. Equal numbers were lifted from misery. Children lived better than their parents. Education became a common treasure, as did better health. And the gifts of innumerable cultures, together with the amazing discoveries of science and inventions of technology, moved far beyond their home borders.

At the same time, the Nineteenth Century's domestic problems of industrializing nations have now gone global with a vengeance. Mass unemployment, severe cyclical slumps in rapid-fire investment and mobile business, the spreading distance between rich and poor in a confrontation of limousine plenty and homelessness in the same streets, and limited revenues for limitless needs now afflict most all societies, even if in drastically different proportion.

Still, there may be a difference of 2007 from 1907 beyond that of scale. If so, it rests somewhere near the intersection of The Big Economy (the global human economy) with The Great Economy (the economy of nature).[12] Local human economies have been reduced to complications of trans-national decisions, or simply left aside altogether. Governance efforts themselves either ally with or are pulled apart by transnational economic forces as the latter exercise political influence as well as economic power. Revolutions in communications and transport annihilate time and distance and invade traditional communities and their ways of life, very often in destructive ways. And hardly anyone truly believes that present institutions have control over the collective consequences of The Big Economy[13] on the planet.

At the same time a phenomenon the Nineteenth Century never conceived strides front and center to qualify everything. This is human power, chiefly techno-economic power ratcheted by factors of growing affluence and population, sufficient to outstrip earth's capacity to restore itself on terms hospitable to life as we know it. So we are now witnessing the revenge of The Great Economy (the economy of nature) as The Big Economy bears down upon it and sometimes ravages it. Its revenge is to withhold its fecundity and to balk in its own cycles of regeneration and renewal; in short, to write "unsustainable" for "sustainable" over the habitat of its own flora and fauna, human fauna included. So at the beginning of the Twentieth Century, soil erosion was not exceeding soil formation (or at least we didn't notice). Species extinction was not exceeding species evolution. Carbon emissions were not exceeding carbon fixation. Fish catches were not exceeding fish reproduction. Forest destruction was not exceeding forest regeneration. Freshwater was not exceeding aquifer replenishment.[14] Half the world's coastlines, the most densely populated human areas, were not imperiled. Nor was anything like half the world's human population crowded into urban areas, with fewer chances for self-sustainability than people on the land have when times turn desperate. Thus there appear at century's close words largely unknown at century's beginning: "unsustainability," "carrying capacity," "the integrity of creation," and "sustainable development." More importantly, the reality at century's end that virtually every natural system essential to The Big Economy was in a state of slow degradation was not the reality at century's onset. (Or if it was it was not recognized.) The economy of nature was not yet fighting the human economy, even when the latter was treating the whole world as game and booty and landfill. Western-based globalization had not yet reached into every nook and cranny with economic practices that didn't much bother to ask what nature's economy requires for its own regeneration and renewal.

But where do we go from here?

One necessary change pertains to the frameworks and notions within which we think, the categories we "think with" when we "think about" things (to recall E. F. Schumacher's distinctions). Here Juergen Moltmann's testimony is significant. Moltmann reconsiders his career, only to conclude: "If I could start all over again, I would link my theology with ecological economics. The last two centuries were dominated by economic questions; the next century will be the age of ecology, in which the organism of the earth will become the all-determining factor and will have to be taken into consideration by everyone."[15]

This is another way of saying what was asserted above: the crucial issues before us lie at the intersection of The Big Economy and The Great Economy, compounded profoundly by race, gender, and culture. But Moltmann's specific point is that the dialogue partner for theology shifts from philosophy and the social sciences to ecological economics. Moltmann's point, put differently, is that theology must turn to thinking within a framework "in which the organism of the earth will become the all-determining factor." Just finding the categories to do so entails a theological reimagining that can only be compared with the reconstruals of great reformations! Here is the paradigm shift asked for but not yet accomplished: How do we do all our theological reflection from earth-centered praxis, with "Earth" encompassing the human economy and the economy of [the rest of] nature together? How do we shift in our understanding and articulation of faith from anthropocentric and androcentric categories and habits to biocentric and geocentric frames? How do we articulate Christian vocation as quite simply fidelity to Earth, and measure all our religious and moral impulses by the criterion of their contribution to Earth's care and well-being? (With "Earth" again understood as comprehensive of nature and society together as a single, complex community full of life but "under house arrest," to recall the word of Boutros Boutros-Ghali at the 1992 Earth Summit.)

The Plowshares Institute report, *Changing The Way Seminaries Teach: Globalization and Theological Education*, is not sanguine about this shift. The report is restricted to the study of twelve North American seminaries that participated in the Globalization of Theological Education program over five years in the early 1990s. The research conclusions nonetheless likely pertain to far more institutions than this slender dozen. One conclusion is that in a time when "multi-national, corporate capitalism" is "one, if not *the*, major causal force behind global interdependence," North American seminary education has given "little theological attention . . . to economics in general and global capitalism in particular."[16] Furthermore, attention to ecological issues does not warrant notice at all, much less the huge agenda that sits where the globalizing economy and planetary life systems rub raw against each other. The report documents in detail the need for a new "conceptual space" for theological education and argues for it. Yet "the organism of earth" as the "all-determining factor" is not conceived *as* that conceptual space in the report. It is still missing in action as the framework within which the theological enterprise does what it does for people of faith.

If we *did* make the global economy and the economy of nature together key concerns for the conceptual space of theological work, what would need to happen beyond Moltmann's nomination of a new dialogue partner? If the Spirit of the Twentith Century were to contemplate "why [this century's great developments] have been so," where would that Spirit turn?

It is easiest to say where such consideration has *not* occurred. Again, my reference point is North America, specifically the United States. While it is easy to make the case that economic globalization, under the impact of the Information Revolution, involves the most fundamental redesign and centralization of economic power since the Industrial Revolution, with far-reaching consequences for political power, and while it is easy to document how swiftly planetary life systems have been placed in jeopardy, it is difficult to find the major institutions of society attending to these in any but superficial ways. That is, it is difficult to find those institutions that know and show the "ecological," "social," and "economic" interconnections *from the inside out*. Neither the mass media, nor government, nor corporations help us understand their interiority. None of them explains, in Jerry Mander's words,

> that all these issues—overcrowded cities, unusual
> and disturbing new weather patterns, the growth
> of global poverty, the lowering of wages while stock
> prices soar, the elimination of social services, the
> destruction of wildlife and wilderness, the protests

of Maya Indians in Mexico—are products of the same global policies. They are all connected to the same economic-political restructuring now under way in the name of accelerated free trade and globalization.[17]

About the only force trying to uncover truth and speak it to power is the loose network of Non-Governmental Organizations (NGOs) that operate locally, regionally, and, by increasing measure, globally. Here something is clearly afoot. What is afoot is backlash against the forces of globalization. What is afoot are efforts to preserve what is endangered by globalization. These only partially organized efforts are largely "off-camera," to be sure, but they are widespread. They include local citizens' movements and alternative institutions that are trying to create greater economic self-sufficiency; sustain livelihoods; work out agriculture appropriate to regions; preserve traditions, languages, and cultures; revive religious life; repair the moral and social fiber; resist the commodification of all things; internalize costs to the Earth in the price of goods; protect ecosystems; and cultivate a sense of Earth as a sacred good held in common. Churches and movements, especially those active in ecumenical networks, are significant participants here, even when their activities have not yet been placed at the center of theological education itself. Richard Barnet and John Cavanagh, who judge this inchoate NGO uprising as presently "the only force we see that can break the global gridlock," finish their important study with a judgment about its high stakes: "The great question of our age is whether people, acting with the spirit, energy, and urgency our collective crisis requires, can develop a democratic global consciousness rooted in authentic local communities."[18]

"A democratic global consciousness rooted in authentic local communities" is, of course, another way—albeit a modern one—to express one version of the ancient ecumenical vision itself! The church in every place *is* the church universal and the church universal is legitimately represented in each place. Yet what churches face as the grave issues at the onset of this century is the same as all other communities face: the compelling need to understand "the organism of the earth" as "the all-determining factor" that is presently endangered; the need to understand that Earth—nature and society together—is a comprehensive community itself, one without an exit; the need to understand faith now as fidelity to Earth in accord with creation's integrity as God-given.

To track ecumenical Christianities as Earth faiths and see which practices prefigure faith as fidelity to Earth, I have devised a research agenda whose centerpiece is site visits done simultaneously with a re-reading of the "deep traditions" of Christian faith. That is described as Part II below. Here I only sort and name further elements of Part I that are important to Part II and introduced by the foregoing commentary.

Further treatment of Part I will describe, in the form of historical narrative and eco-social analysis, the transformations of nature/culture that have occurred across the three waves of globalization. The contributions of this way of giving an account "of the humankind we left to thee" are twofold. First, it will, "from below," expose the continuities of the waves of conquest and colonization, development, and free trade global capitalism. These peregrinations of globalization are different chapters of the same tale, though it is a tale rarely told in that fashion by those who write the reigning historical accounts. But from the perspective of peoples and lands that have suffered, the continuities are graphic. Second, it will show that nature and culture are never separated; society and the land are always transformed together. Yet phrases like "the biological expansion of Europe" or "ecological imperialism" (Alfred Crosby) strike moderns as odd. The reason is that we live by conceptual distinctions—of nature and history, society and nature, people and the land, human beings and nature—that systematically filter out actual, effective relationships and their world-altering impact. We lack the means to perceive and conceive Earth as a comprehensive community and instead push on in apartheid fashion, regarding ourselves as an ecologically segregated species.

Into this narrative description of the world as transformed by global economic and environmental forces two further accounts will be woven.

One is the role of Christianity. Much has been done here and I will not go to great length to repeat the fact that too few voices in dominating North Atlantic Christianities have been raised against the global political expansion that represented the greatest demographic change and land transfer and transformation in the history of the world (European emigration and the settling of neo-

Europes around the world, coupled with white supremacy). Nor have many voices been raised against economic domination in the form of globalizing industrialism as led by capitalism. It is probably necessary to say, but not in detail, that Protestant churches in particular have been closely aligned with the rise of the bourgeoisie in the eighteenth century and have helped maintain the hegemony of that class and of white supremacy in the nineteenth and twentieth centuries. More important for the project overall is to turn from the fallacy of Christianity as a European religion and neo-European civilization as Christian to the multiple histories of Christianities whose experience of modernity is not one of strong alliance and tepid critique, but whose experience includes the impact of globalization. Hence I will visit communities of Africa and Asia (Copts, Mar Thoma Church) who address Earth issues from traditions that do not belong to European/American cultural history. Or I will visit communities of indigenous-based Christianity who may have been the target of missionary activity but whose Christianity has come to tap other, native roots (The Association of African Earthkeeping Churches, for example). And I will visit communities that have multiple cultural and historical roots that include Euro-American influences and local, indigenous histories (The Khanya Programme of the Methodist Church in the Eastern Cape, South Africa, and the Orthodox Church in Alaska). To these I will add visits to dissenting communities of the North Atlantic and the Americas, communities that are challenging dominant Christianities through a selective use of older traditions in the cause of present renewal, renewal that adds up to Christianity as an Earth faith (The Iona Community in Scotland is one example, faith-based community organizing in North American cities is another when it addresses social and environmental issues together). Through such an account of multiple Christianities I intend to set the stage not only for the site visits of Part II, but for the effort in Part III to expose the viability and richness of Christian traditions and identities for rooted contributions to present Earth community and an Earth ethic.

The other narrative in Part I is an account of the moral life as framed and experienced in the centuries of globalization. This will focus on the grounding rationale of morality and ethics, especially Christian explications, and the linkages of these to normative moralities carried with globalizing forces. There is, for example, an important and complex relationship of European Christian natural law morality to the treatment of indigenous peoples of the Americas and Australia. The connection to the "law of discovery" that became enshrined in Western legal thought is especially important. But so are other, i.e., non-natural law, notions of Christian morality that accompany the *mission civilisatrice*. The Kantian and utilitarian traditions, for example, have consistently drawn the boundaries of the moral universe around humans only (and some humans more than others!) and have thus been virtually blind to consequences of human action on the other-than-human world (*i.e.*, most of the world).

Part I, then, uses analysis and narrative centered in the transformation of nature/culture over the past five centuries, in order to say where we are presently and why. The centerpiece is the interaction of the global human economy and the economy of nature as portrayed by successive waves of globalization. Secondary themes are the narratives of Christianities and reigning moralities in this context and period.

Part II Site Visits and Deep Traditions

The centerpiece of this section are site visits to self-identified Christian earth-keeping communities. The communities have been selected in keeping with criteria listed below. Each chapter of Part II will include a description of the setting of the community, its makeup and its practices, and an explication of its theo-ethical "world." The significance for community spiritual-moral formation beyond the boundaries of the site visited will also be noted. Finally—this is a major discussion in each chapter—the ties of this living community to "deep traditions" of Christian faith will be made (see below). These deep traditions are sacramental communion, mysticism/contemplation, ascetic community, and prophetic/liberative practices. (Any given site may express several of these in their practices and self-understanding. My point is not to fit communities into a typology but to show the contours of the Christian moral life that follow from tradition-formed elements.)

Specifically, each of the site visit chapters will include:
- some visuals (artwork, space arrangements, worship materials, etc.)

- a key quotation or two that captures the chapter and leads off
- descriptive accounts of present form/examples (observer as narrator)
- the biblical and historical "feet" or "roots" (usually supplied by the communities themselves)
- theo-ethical rationale, together with details of the practices that address eco-justice issues
- contribution to community moral formation and a spiritual-moral universe for just and sustainable communities; included here are
- intimations of the way this living tradition meets the elements of Part I and offers an alternative (e.g., sacramentalism vs. the utterly desacralized, commoditized, and utilitarian way of the globalized economy; asceticism as a way of loving the earth fiercely in a simple way of life that says "no" to consumerism and "yes" to shared life together; etc.).

The criteria used to select communities/practices/traditions include these:

- cultivated sensibilities for "eco-justice" and conscious connections of these to the practice of Christian faith;
- accessibility: can we talk with persons, describe their communities and work, and use available documentation?
- would participants be willing to respond to a "brief" of this Luce Project as part of the research conversation? (this would include key categories and goals)
- would participants permit materials to be published, including artwork, sketches of facilities, core beliefs, descriptions of practices, etc.? (There would be reciprocity for this—a teaching session on site, copies of later publications, etc.—as well as reimbursement for all expenses incurred in hosting the research.)
- do participants, overall, represent a wide spectrum of Christian traditions and understand themselves as expressions of living traditions and/or transformations of them?
- do participants, overall, represent different locales (rural/urban, One-Third and Two-Thirds Worlds, e.g.) and different racial-ethnic, class, and cultural mixes?

The substance of the deep Christian traditions I will re-read in conjunction with site visits will be arrived at inductively, at least in part. That is, my visit to the Coptic monasteries of Wadi al-Natrun in the Desert of Scetis, Upper Egypt, concentrated on the ways of the desert fathers and mothers and the traditions and theologies of asceticism. Time with the Maryknoll Sisters in Baguio City, the Philippines, drew them out on their use of Roman Catholic sacramentalism and contemplation, and sought the influence of "the new creation story" as revelation (Thomas Berry) on their work, together with the influence of the popular Catholic cosmology of the Cordillera mountain peoples. All of which is to say that I will listen carefully to the traditions expressed in these living communities and describe them, with a view to traditions that have formed these communities and shaped their identity and mission. The inductive task is critical, because I am not simply assuming that my selection and re-reading of deep traditions will necessarily correspond to what I, in fact, find.

That said, I have taken and will take along informed notions of the traditions the communities self-identify as important, and I have and will look especially for the Earth-oriented or potentially Earth-oriented elements of these traditions. All of the traditions are as old as Christianity itself and sometimes older (in pre-Christian forms that influenced Christianity). And all can be, I assume, potential materials for "the great work" of the age[19]—namely, fashioning Earth-friendly ways of life, including Earth-inclusive thought-frames, so that the relationship of human ways to the rest of nature's are mutually enhancing. At the same time, the nature of "the great work" means that I will bring a specific normative question; namely, insofar as need be, can these traditions themselves be converted to Earth and recast so as to help wed justice to sustainability? My present short-hand version of these traditions, together with a brief assessment, is as follows.

Community asceticism. There have always been religious communities as communities of renunciation and annunciation. "No" is said to one way of life, "yes" to another. Strains of asceticism discipline the ego and the will and nurture a life of virtue that counters a life of distracting attachments, ostentation, conspicuous consumption, and loose sex. Differently said, asceticism seeks to forge a counterworld nurtured by an alternative ethos. Monasticism is one obvious strand in Orthodox, Roman Catholic, and Anglican communions, but ascetic Protestant communities show similar traits, especially communities of the Radical Reformation. A close look uncovers both the life of renunciation and a simultaneous effort to embody harmony with nature as manifest in clothing and diet, agricultural and healing practices, art and architecture. In recent decades covenanting communities in urban areas have also undertaken to do what ascetic Christian community has always sought to do: reject as normative the dominant culture of its surrounding world while at the same time embodying an alternative in the details of its own simple and disciplined life, details that include the treatment of nature and the just ordering of human relationships as matters of "daily bread."

I add that ascetic commitment is a deep tradition not only in Christianity where it has been present in some form in every century of Christianity's two millennia; it is a standard feature of most religious traditions. That is not a small matter or a throwaway line. It is a kind of criterion of selection. For something as far-reaching as the needed religious conversion to Earth, we should be instinctively ecumenical and seek traditions that not only have seniority but are also widespread in human experience.

The *kind* of asceticism most needed now is one that loves the Earth fiercely in a simple way of life, with disciplined and heightened senses for God's presence in all of life. As an Indian friend puts it in her lament about what is happening to many Indians: We are trading an Indian focus on a simple way of life and high thought for a cluttered way and low thought.[20]

A necessary gloss on ascetic community would go like the following: Christian asceticism's own conversion to Earth requires that it abandon a metaphysic it has borne and treasured most of its days. Namely, the Christian life lived out of the metaphor of ascetic ascent, life lived in a hard scramble upward on the Great Chain of Being. Here the closer one is to God the more Earth is left behind; the deeper the communion with God, the lighter our embrace of the creaturely; the more the indwelling of the Spirit, the less attentive our senses are to the world around; the more our passion for God, the less our passion for Earthly life. What, then, are the practices of an asceticism that loves the Earth fiercely in a simple way of life, as the way of loving God fiercely? This becomes the lead question for conversion in both practice and theory.

Sacramental communion is another ancient and living tradition. In the sacramentalist tradition, life in its totality is brought into the worshipful presence of God. There it is renewed in contemplative and sacramental practices. Life is a gift of God and the medium of grace. Far more than a gathering of God and humankind, sacramental communion is ritually enacted community as the hymn of the universe itself. Its great acts are acts of the cosmic drama of creation and its story is one that proclaims a God beyond dimensions we can know, yet as near as the grain and the grape, the water and the oil. Creation and its transfiguration, together with human salvation, is the great theme here, whether in Orthodox communions, Celtic Christianity, Roman Catholic or Anglican bodies (to mention only some of its Christian variants). While a deep and broad tradition, it is in fact almost the antithesis of the working cosmology and theology of the institutions and practices that created the modern world. Modern institutions and practices have assumed a plastic view of nature characterized simply as "natural resources." "Natural resources" and capital, like "human resources" and "human capital," betray a mindset that is utilitarian with a vengeance and utterly devoid of any sacramental sense. They belong to a disenchanted world where the numinous is beaten from the common and the sacred leached from the ordinary.

A necessary gloss on sacramental communion as potentially Earth-enhancing would include several matters. One is the continuing legacy of its Middle Age and Reformation preoccupation with human salvation as *the* focus. By contrast, the proper circumference is the redemption of *all* creation as the abode of God. The Orthodox and Anglican communions are sometimes better in their reach here. All nature is transfigured in the Orthodox eucharist, for example. But they continue, like Rome and many Protestants, to invest the celebration of the sacraments themselves with a church order governed by that other deep and enduring tradition, patriarchy. So all nature is transfigured, with the notable exception of male-dominated church order! Nor can the metaphysics of sacramentalism continue to be that of "Greek" substance metaphysics. Rather, the theological work now in this tradition is to offer an evolutionary sacramentalist ontology that resonates with the story of the cosmos itself on its own stunning pilgrimage.

Community mysticism / contemplation is another long-standing practice or set of practices that reach across diverse Christianities and other faiths. This orientation and these practices all rest in the conviction that "we can touch with our living hearts the Heart of the World and listen to the secret revelations of its unending beat,"[21] and that we can do so in ways that transcend the hold that forces around us have upon us. Here is the attempt, made innumerable times by millions over thousands of years, to "move beyond the confines of society and history, to break the bounds of normal human interaction, normal consciousness, and normal physical reality"[22] in order to draw from a wisdom hidden within this world or resident beyond it. The struggle is always between such transcending wisdom and the powers around us. Like asceticism, here is momentary release from the grip of the social ego and the socially constructed sense of the body itself; here is direct, if temporary, experience of the divine beyond the definitions of dogma, institution, even moral stipulation; here is truth apprehended apart from the authority of society's keepers of the truth; and here is revelation itself as shorn from our attachments and mistaken yearnings. Self falls away, the heresy of "mine" and "thine" falls away as well, and the vision quest of the mystic ends in the cool cosmic fire some name "God" and others refuse to name at all. And when the return is made, as it must, and intransigent worldly reality insinuates itself all over again, the mystical community finds itself so identified with a cosmic beauty and harmony that it is permanently dissatisfied with the world around. It may "accept" that world in one sense—namely, embrace it with compassion. But that world will not be right until it is Eden reborn and its energies sing with the stars. So the mystical community backs into strong moral agency with no sense of heteronomous obligation at all, only the overflow of hearts that cannot deny their moment with God and the wondrous burden of their experience of beauty and truth.

Most Christian mysticism is not, it should be added, of the present popular varieties. That is, most Christian mysticism is not mysticism turned toward the human subject itself, with high recollection of "my" feelings and state. It is not the tale of my experience. Rather, most Christian mysticism is the tale of the divine and the appearance of the form and substance of wisdom revealed to me (or to us). Both traditional and modern forms can, of course, be escapes, a forgetting of the people on the block or the mundane tasks in the field, escapes that spiritual mentors commonly warn against, just as they warn against mistaking "Real Error" for "the Great Truth" and using a "Truth Beyond Question" as a means of "Power Over the Uninitiated."[23] The world is always "too much with us" and mature mystics know that this holds for their transcendental moments as well.

What is rarely left behind, even in the strong apophatic tradition of mysticism, is—strikingly—nature. Nature abounds in the mystic's experience and holds uncommonly high rank in mystical visions. God in, as, and through the physical world is often the experience. Take for example Hildegard of Bingen's direct encounter with the divine: "I, the fiery life of divine essence, am aflame beyond the beauty of the meadows, I gleam in the waters, and I burn in the sun, moon, and stars . . . I awaken everything to life." The mystical may happen in the direct encounter with a detail of nature, whether the numinous is named as God or not. Annie Dillard describes a sudden face-to-face moment with a weasel: "Our eyes locked, and someone threw away the key. Our look was as if two lovers, or deadly enemies, met unexpectedly on an overgrown path when each had been thinking of something else." Aldo Leopold, too, cannot forget the eyes, the "fierce green fire" in the eyes of a dying wolf he himself had just shot. Never again, he said, could he think of wolves, or mountains, or wilderness in the same way.[24]

The mystical/contemplative tradition, then, may or may not mediate Christian faith as Earth faith. It may or may not be life-charged mysticism. But it certainly can be and is for some, with great power. For others, however, nature and Earth serve as means on a journey that leaves them behind as useful but now discarded cumber. As an Earth faith this tradition and set of practices is no more pristine than asceticism or sacramentalism.

Prophetic / liberative community practice is yet another effort to articulate fidelity to God as fidelity to Earth. For the Hebrew prophets, redemption is the redemption of all creation, human and non-human, history and nature together. When "the vines languish, the merry-hearted sigh." When "the city . . . is broken down . . . the gladness of earth is banished." (Isaiah 24) This is liberation of all life, from the cell to the community, a struggle inclusive of the poor, the weak, the marginalized, the diseased and disfigured, exploited and exhausted nature. The God of mercy and compassion, who is also Judge, "knows" their suffering and goes before in the journey to a teeming land and fertile Sabbath. This prophetic tradition took on a certain decisive shape in the modern period itself, in the face of "the social question" that modernity generated. Aided by social theory and social scientific analysis of society, it adopted direct efforts to refashion institutions, systems, structures, and policies in the direction of shared and saving power. It shifted Christian ethics from an overwhelmingly virtue-oriented ethic (of asceticism, sacramentalism, and mysticism) to a value-oriented ethic that seeks to realize social goods directly by attending to how we pattern human behavior through institutions, policies, and practices. It tries to fashion a social order that makes it easier for people to do and to be good—and harder for them to be and do evil. The Social Gospel, Christian Realism, liberation, and socio-ecological theologies all belong to recent versions of this ancient moral tradition, as does progressive evangelicalism.

The gloss here need not deter us long. What is needed is chiefly a matter of overcoming the remaining anthropocentrism in justice-focused traditions. Or, to recall our earlier terms, what is needed is an account of responsibility that encompasses the sociocommunal, biophysical, and geoplanetary when the moral universe of much Christian ethics in this very tradition has drawn the line around human populations alone and understood issues of power to be intrahuman only.

Overall this sketch does not add up to a template. These four streams of traditions illustrate long-standing, highly variegated, diverse and suggestive strands that might yet serve what is of necessity an *imaginative* realization of conceptual frameworks and spiritual-moral formation adequate to the next period of history. It is only a crude map, not the territory itself. Still, it offers one possible orientation for the collective work we face and a suggestive way to engage living communities who identify their socio-eco work with these traditions.

Part III The Contribution of Christian Earth Faiths

Overall, Part III will draw out the meaning and significance of Part II visits and elaborate these in view of the world presented in Part

I. In the book it will do so in three or four chapters. One chapter will restate the necessity of addressing transformed nature and society together (the "social question" and the "ecological question" as the justice-and-sustainability imperative alive for the foreseeable future). A quick recall of this reality as experienced in each of the site locations will be used, as well as other examples from different locales (a number of these will represent congregation-based activity in the U.S. and Canada). This chapter will also sketch a spiritual-moral "world" that is the author's reflection on the project overall. This "world" will be evident as an expression of varied Christianities as Earth faiths, expressing the "deep traditions" met and elaborated in the plural communities visited. A subsequent chapter will focus more tightly on contributions for community moral formation/public policy in the interest of sustainable communities. The notion is to lay out the *tasks* of moral formation, both civic and ecclesial, and the *substance* offered by various Christianities as Earth faiths, substance borne above all in exemplary *practices*. The next chapter will address theory and method in Christian ethics itself. This is a constructive statement of the research results for moral theory (non-anthropocentric, socio-environmental theory out of rooted practices that inform further future policies, transdisciplinary, interstructured moral analysis done collaboratively, etc). In short, this is a chapter on the kind of moral analysis and framework the research has used and leads to, some reflection on this, and a recommendation of it for persons and communities removed from the sites visited. Again, the purpose is to offer an alternative to the moral categories and worlds portrayed in Part I. To illustrate how such moral theory would work in the interests of an Earth ethic grounded in both religious and secular moral theory, I may add a chapter that transforms the present rationale for universal human rights in such a way as to include current work on the Earth Charter. The results would be environmental or biotic rights integrally related with human rights, i.e., the whole Community of Life would be the subject of a shared moral "universe."

Endnotes

1.   Dietrich Bonhoeffer, "Grundfragen einer christlichen Ethik," *Gesammelte Schriften* (Munchen: C. Kaiser, 1966), 3:56; trans. mine.

2.   Dale Irvin, *Christian Histories, Christian Traditioning: Rendering Accounts* (Maryknoll: Orbis Books, 1998), 129.

3.   The reference is to the book of Belden C. Lane, *The Solace of Fierce Landscapes: Exploring Desert and Mountain Spirituality* (New York: Oxford University Press, 1998).

4.   In Dorothee Soelle's words: "The tradition that joins us together is justice. 'God is the universe,' 'God is the maker of the cosmos,' 'God is energy,' 'God is the light'— I can say all that, too. But, coming from the Judeo-Christian tradition, I must first say, God is justice. To know God means to do justice." Dorothee Soelle, *Against the Wind: Memoir of a Radical Christian,* trans. by Barbara and Martin Rumscheidt (Minneapolis: Fortress Press, 1999), 103.

5.   I am indebted to Vandana Shiva for this suggestion; see her book, *Biopiracy: The Plunder of Nature and Knowledge* (Toronto: Between the Lines Press, 1997).

6.   Walter Rauschenbusch, *Christianity and the Social Crisis* (New York: The Macmillan Co., 1907), 211.

7.   Ibid., 211.

8.   Ibid., 211.

9.   Ibid., 212.

10.   Ibid., 212.

11.   Ibid., 212.

12.   The phrases, "The Big Economy" and "The Great Economy," are Wendell Berry's.

13.   For a detailed account of these and other dynamics, see Eric J. Hobsbawm, *The Age of Extremes: A History of the World, 1914-1991* (New York: Pantheon Books, 1994).

14.   See Lester R. Brown, Hal Kane, and David Malin Roodman, *Vital Signs, 1994: The Trends That Are Shaping Our Future* (New York and London: W. W. Norton & Co., 1994), 15-21.

15.   Juergen Moltmann, "The Adventure of Theological Ideas," as cited in M. Douglas Meeks, "Juergen Moltmann's *Systematic Contributions to Theology,*" *Religious Studies Review*, Vol. 22, No. 2 (1996): 105.

16.   David A. Roozen, Alice Frazier Evans, and Robert A. Evans, *Changing the Way Seminaries Teach: Globalization and Theological Education* (Hartford: Hartford Seminary Center for Social and Religious Research, 1966), 189-190.

17.   Jerry Mander, "The Dark Side of Globalization: What the Media Are Missing," *The Nation*, Vol. 263, No. 3 (1996): 12.

18.   Richard J. Barnet and John Cavanaugh, *Global Dreams: Imperial Corporations and the New World Order* (New York: Simon and Schuster, 1994), 430.

19.   Comments by Thomas Berry at the Christianity & Ecology Conference, Harvard Center for the Study of World Religions, April 16, 1998.

20.   The comment of Nafisa Goga D'Souza in her address at the conference on "Global Eco-Justice and the Church's Urban Mission," Lutheran School of Theology, Chicago, April 23, 1998.

21.   Roger Gottlieb, "The Transcendence of Justice and the Justice of Transcendence: Mysticism, Deep Ecology, and Political Life," *Journal of the American Academy of Religion*, Vol. 67, No. 1 (1999): 149.

22.   Ibid., 150.

23.   Ibid., 153. I draw consistently upon Gottlieb for this discussion of mysticism.

24.   These quotations and the discussion are taken from Gottlieb, "The Transcendence of Justice and the Justice of Transcendence," 155-156.

Liturgical Aesthetics and Kenotic Receptivity

Don E. Saliers
CANDLER SCHOOL OF THEOLOGY
OF EMORY UNIVERSITY
ATLANTA, GEORGIA

> Look at the liturgy: among the forms of Christian art, it is the transcendent and dominant one; the Spirit of God . . . formed it, in order to have pleasure in it . . . . The beauty of the liturgy belongs among the glorious gifts of God which are granted us when we seek the kingdom of God. In any other instances, the liturgy becomes a spectacle and a sin.[1]

Can Christian liturgy still form and sustain human dispositions to acknowledge, perceive, and live in the world as the arena of God's glory? Is this possible in a culture dominated by entertainment, immediacy of feeling, manipulated desire, and forgetfulness of being? What is this "beauty" in liturgical life of which van der Leeuw speaks so readily? These are questions that theology must address when the practices of Christian worship are under scrutiny as they are in our age. Such questions are a pathway into theological aesthetics, and in particular to this essay in "liturgical aesthetics."

The history of Christian faith and theology is also a history of the eye, the ear, of bodily gesture and movement, the mind imagining, and the senses conjoining. Wherever human beings hear and encounter the divine, the consequences are poetic, visionary, metaphoric, parabolic, and ordered sound—voices, instruments, and dance. Central to Christian faith and life are the practices of worship. The poetry of hymns and psalms and spiritual songs arises in the earliest worshiping assemblies. The common elements of earth, air, fire, and water, and the fruits of earth and human work—oil, wheat become bread, grapes become wine, ordered sound and visual form—all take on symbolic and communicative power when used in Christian worship.

Theological aesthetics keeps returning to primary practices that constitute worship of God. Despite all temptations to the contrary, Christianity steadfastly remains a religion of the body: Christ incarnate, the Word's body crucified, risen, proclaimed, and enacted in rituals of the common meal in his name. From the beginning Christian communities have forged and transformed human ideas of the common good, as well as the beautiful, in and through central ritual activities. Such rituals, with few exceptions, are permeated with human arts, requiring receptivity of human senses and intellect. Suspicion of the arts in worship arises when the power of the sensory is deemed to lead to idolatry, or when it leads only to self-absorption.[2] This is why the church must continually reflect on the means by which the divine/human transaction called "liturgy" takes place. If the music of heaven became the music of earth, and the Word of God was heard and made visible, then the aesthetics and the poetics of worship are crucial to the continual work of theology. As David Power has observed, "In the realm of the holy, the poetic must win out." For it is the "poetic [that] must integrate the tragic and the comic of life with a vision of the future."[3]

Current debates and collisions of sensibility concerning worship in North American contexts now bring these considerations into the arena of pastoral practice and everyday life for many Christian traditions. Hence the need for liturgical theology to provide a framework for rethinking the aesthetic dimensions of worship and the "poetics" of liturgical participation. While questions of holiness and beauty have always accompanied discourse about God, especially in periods heavily influenced by Platonic and Neo-Platonic sources, our present situation in church and culture renders such questions fragmented and problematic. The very terms "aesthetics," "beauty," and "holiness" are now very much contested.

This essay aims to set an agenda for liturgical aesthetics. Six "tensive" theses will be advanced and explored, with a particular eye toward a theory I shall call the *kenotic aesthetic of Christian liturgy*. While strong differences among Christian worshiping traditions are to be acknowledged, I hope this agenda also suggests a broadly ecumenical framework for addressing a range of current theological and liturgical issues well beyond the scope of a single essay.

Beauty and Holiness: Primary Ambivalence

Von Balthasar has remarked, "In a world without beauty . . . in a world which is perhaps not wholly without beauty, but which can no longer see it or reckon with it: in such a world the good also loses its attractiveness, the self-evidence of why it must be carried out."[4] In working out a theological aesthetics on the basis of divine reve-latory initiative, von Balthasar seeks to show the inner connection between the beautiful and the good, between the aesthetic and the ethical. Receptivity toward what is beautiful is crucial to the abil-ity to envision and do what is good. Works of art can be said to die, in his view, under a dull and uncomprehending human gaze, so " . . . even the radiance of holiness can . . . become blunted when it encounters nothing but hollow indifference."[5] This suggests why we might focus on active receptivity toward the beautiful and the good in Christian worship. Without the aesthetic embodied in communal practices, the vision of goodness grounded in the holiness of God may lose its point.

But Christian theology has shown a long and studied ambiva-lence toward human aesthetic capacities, and especially toward re-lationships between art and religious faith. On the one hand beauty has been included among the transcendental ingredients in classi-cal theology, often linked with reasoning to and about God by anal-ogy. On the other hand, prophetic strands in Judaism and Chris-tianity have regarded the human imagination with suspicion, gen-erating historical periods of strident iconoclasm. Idolatry and the distractions of sensuality are two main polemical targets of such religious critique. Yet God's glory, and the goodness and beauty of the created order of heaven and earth, are perennial subjects of praise and acknowledgment in Christian public worship. Doxology is central to naming God, just as lament over the broken and the unlovely features of human life and the world is needed for pro-phetic and truthful worship. Doing justice and mercy in the face of human distortion and death is the impulse when lament and doxol-ogy meet in worship.

With such ambivalence we must begin. This is not simply be-cause of the Platonic and Neo-Platonic cautions against substitut-ing beauty and pleasure for the pursuit of true virtue and faith in

God. Ambivalence is built into the message of Christianity. The symbol of the cross and the claim that God in Christ assumed sin and death create a necessary tension internal to Christian revelation itself. Thus any consideration of how Christian liturgy should employ aesthetic means cannot concentrate naively on beauty by itself. Many theologians in the long history of theology have claimed that the wonders of created beauty can and ought to lead human beings toward God, the Source of all goodness and beauty. However, running alongside this theme sounded in the creation psalms and the great Eucharistic prayers of the church, East and West, is the theme of human sin and the distortions of a fallen creation. Whatever eros toward beauty we assume, and whatever human artistic powers may be, the self-giving of God in the life, passion, death, and resurrection of Christ stands against all tendencies toward idolatry and human self-absorption.

If liturgical aesthetics is to illuminate relations between the beauty and goodness of God mediated by liturgical events, it must do so by naming original ambivalences as well. This may prove especially important to the current situation originating in so-called "culture wars" among and with Christian churches today. The inability to make mature theological assessments of various artistic media today is due, in part, to uncritical assumptions about the concepts before us: beauty, goodness, and holiness. Debates about what is appropriate in worship too often devolve into unreflective appeals to "taste" and cultural preferences.[6]

Among the tasks of liturgical theology is the explication of the "primary theology" of a given worshiping assembly. Such primary theology is itself shaped by and expressed by aesthetic means. Here "aesthetic" refers both to the forms of perception and to the qualities of particular words, symbols, gestures, and visual and aural forms. In other words, the aesthetic requires attention to what gains attention, is received as beautiful, etc. This is at once a theoretical and a practical discipline.

What Christian Liturgy Requires

For several years in the 1960s and early 1970s my family and I lived in a city neighborhood. Our four daughters, then quite young, were taught a set of ritual songs by the neighborhood children. They would gather to form a circle and, calling out to one another across twirling jump ropes, would begin to sing and move. One at a time, and occasionally in pairs, the children would dance into the circle, hop a few steps, then dance away all the time singing amid the whirling ropes: "Miss Mary Mack, Mack, Mack, all dressed in black, black, black, with silver buttons, buttons, buttons, all down her back, back, back . . . ." This ritual game gave pleasure and conferred identity to participants and observers alike.

That dancing, singing image of the children still sheds light on matters of aesthetics and poetics in Christian worship. They learned the rhythms, words, and rules in and through their participation. The circling song and movements were improvisational, sometimes strikingly so, but the rules were clearly shared by all. The song had to have the right accent in order for the dance to take place. The delight, the physical energy, and the seriousness of the children were evident, yet marked by surprises. One could say that all were conjoined in the ruled freedom of the play. The combination of seriousness, rules, and the play is reminiscent of Romano Guardini's famous definition of liturgy: it is "holy play."[7] The children's ritual play suggests that the aesthetics of religious ritual cannot be divorced from the poetics, the actual participation of human beings in the "making" of the event experienced in the liturgical assembly. To this we shall return.

Christian assemblies for the worship of God require ordered sound, sight, space, movement, gesture, symbolic acts, and sacred texts. The meaning and point of language used to address God and the assembly depends radically on the non-linguistic forms and practices for its formative and expressive power. Paradoxically, all such culturally embedded phenomena must also transcend the given specific culture of the assembly, if God is to be properly addressed. This is why, despite widely varying Christian traditions of worship, I propose that liturgical action itself is best understood as an eschatological art.[8]

Events of Christian worship, while not always "liturgical" in the narrow sense of adhering to a set of prescribed prayers and ritual actions, are communal actions in which the participants are engaged in shared practices aimed at the glorification of God and upbuilding of the community in faith and love. Liturgies are thus not "works of art" to be admired, but communal acts aimed at communion with the divine. Thus the divine/human dialogue in Word and in sacrament, faithfully celebrated, is simultaneously aesthetic and theological. But this is precisely why Christian liturgy requires a series of tensions and juxtapositions, verbal and non-verbal.[9] Theological reflection, born of liturgical participation, on God's glory and on relationships between beauty and holiness must always confront the "anti-aesthetic" entailed in the passion and death of Christ. The highest pitch of this tension may be found in the liturgy of Holy Week, where the brokenness and pain of Christ's passion and death is juxtaposed with, and yet interpenetrates, the glory of the resurrection.

In this sense we affirm that artistic and aesthetic dimensions of human life are intrinsic to liturgical practices, and hence to theological understanding. In the context of liturgical participation, the poetics and aesthetic dimensions of worship are internally connected to concepts of holiness, goodness, and beauty—divine, and human. But this, as we have observed, plunges us into a set of permanent tensions. We cannot assume that the "beauty of holiness" is self-evident, let alone easily grasped. The ambivalence displayed in Augustine's Confessions is therefore not his alone.

> When I love you, what do I love? Not the body's beauty, nor time's rhythm, nor light's brightness . . . nor song's sweet melodies, nor the fragrance of flowers, lotions, and spices, nor manna and honey, nor the feel of flesh embracing flesh—none of these are what I love when I love my God. And yet, it's something like light, sound, smell, food, and touch that I love when I love my God—the light, voice, food, fragrance, and embrace of my inner self, where a light shines for my soul . . . . That's what I love when I love my God![10]

No one can fail to see how deeply intertwined sensible joy and delight in creaturely things are in Augustine's reflections on worshipful love of God. He was possessed of a sense for what is beautiful, rooted here in a Neo-Platonic conception of reason as eros, but also steeped in the language of doxology born in the psalms and Christian Scriptures. Whether intentionally or not, he cites the sensible stuff of liturgical rites of his day in uttering what love of God is "like." The seeming denial of the bodily, the temporal, and the sensory aspects of religious worship is immediately reforged into the descriptive and ascriptive language of the address of worship.

Augustine's remark suggests what we may call *proto-analogies of beauty*. They arise from participation in liturgical actions. While rooted in human experiences, the analogies are generated in prayer, song, and common ritual. They provide what Barth refers to as "analogies of faith." Rather than providing a basis for reasoning from experience to God, these experiential analogies are dependent upon the intentionality of liturgy as a divine/human transaction. The divine/human exchange is, for Christian theology, dependent upon the divine self-giving. The beauty of God's holy self-giving is a "kenotic" beauty precisely because of the passion and the cross. This is constitutive of any account of a Christian liturgical aesthetics.

A striking passage in Karl Barth's *Church Dogmatics II / 1* speaks of the attraction to the divine beauty. "If we can and must say that God is beautiful, to say this is to say how [God] enlightens and convinces and persuades us." God possesses "this power of attraction . . . which wins and conquers, in the fact that [God] is . . . divinely beautiful, . . . as the unattainable primal beauty, yet really beautiful." God is the "One who gives pleasure, creates desire and renews with enjoyment."[11]

This lies at the heart of any Christian aesthetics, and especially of liturgical aesthetics. Recalling Augustine and other classical theologians' recognition of the role of delight and attraction toward God, Barth also wishes to counter any false "aestheticism" that would make human beauty itself the cause of our knowing and worshiping God. For Barth, as for von Balthasar, God's beauty is subordinated to the glory of God, for God cannot remain the deity and be subject to something metaphysical shared with the created order. For Augustine the issue is ambivalent human subjectivity; for Barth the issue is God's sovereignty and the difference between Creator and the creatures. Von Balthasar saw and appreciated this in Barth, and thus in his own theological work incorporates a revelatory role for both the attraction (beauty) of God's glory, and for the evoked desire at the heart of prayer and worship.

The claim that God is both ground and object of the deepest creaturely desire is, I contend, a necessary basis for the following proposals concerning liturgical aesthetics. If we can speak of Christian liturgy as both "source and summit" of the Christian life, then we must investigate how any particular liturgical assembly forms and gives expression to the appropriate dispositions and participation in glory and the holiness of God. For the Christian faith, both the glory and the holiness require a profoundly kenotic element in experience and in theological thinking.

Six Theses Toward a Christian Liturgical Aesthetic

We are now in a position to consider six theses that bear upon the larger aim of this essay. I intend these to be interrelated. While each may be, and must be, examined on its own, their bearing upon a constructive theory of liturgical aesthetics can only be shown in their relation to one another when studying specific liturgical communities. A brief exposition of each will lead to a concluding proposal concerning "active receptivity" appropriate to a kenotic aesthetic of Christian liturgy. Each thesis contains a number of assumptions and implications that cannot be fully pursued here. My contention is that, in working through these points, the general outline of an adequate theological framework will emerge.

The following theses constitute the foundation for a theory of liturgical aesthetics:

1. Christian liturgy is always culturally embodied and embedded.
2. Christian public worship is an art, but not a work of art; it is, in the words of Aidan Kavanagh, a "performative artful symbolic action."[12]
3. The Christian assembly originates in the liturgy of Jesus Christ, thus requiring the paradoxical character of the "glory of the cross," and the poetic fusion of word and act.
4. Every worshiping assembly requires three interrelated levels of participation: the phenomenal/aesthetic, the ecclesial, and the mystical.
5. Christian liturgy is faithful, authentic, and relevant to the extent it displays a series of permanent tensions.
6. Christian liturgy is an eschatological art requiring active receptivity to the form and content of revelation.

Culturally Embodied and Embedded

To observe that Christian liturgy is culturally embodied and embedded is commonplace, yet the implications of this claim have not always been adequately drawn out. When human beings assemble for worship there is usually speaking, singing, listening, observing, gesturing, movement, and particular ritual actions with particular objects. James F. White once defined worship as "speaking and touching in God's name."[13] This minimalist definition begins with human actions in order to highlight the human stuff internal to the theological character of worship. Whatever is said and sung about the divine, human means of communication are involved. Moreover, such means are products of specific human cultures in particular times and places.

A more classical definition of Christian liturgy speaks of the glorification of God and the sanctification of all that is human and creaturely. Even here we note a co-inherent claim. In the very act of praise and thanksgiving, humanity is subject to being made holy. The ascription of holiness to the divine implies the "being made holy" of those who worship. Despite the tendency to associate such a definition with the sense of the "timeless" and the eternal, the very process of sanctification implies temporality and particularity. Sanctification is not other-worldly; it is social, bodily, historical life.

Thus we cannot analyze or interpret liturgical life without attending to the fact that the language, music, movement, and symbols used in worship are themselves culture-permeated. Each may be spoken of as an "art"—rhetoric, musical performance, gestures, iconography, architecture, and particular objects now given ritual significance—having origins in the social/cultural life of a particular people. Sermons, hymns, prayers, the visual and kinetic dimensions of architectural environments are "aesthetic" spheres of human being and understanding.

The history of Christian worship is also a history of the variable cultural aesthetics (sensibilities) and art forms involved. When, for example, the church moved from persecution to establishment in fourth century Rome, royal court ceremonial became part of certain Roman pontifical rites. When Christianity was presented to American slaves of African descent, the art and the aesthetics of song and rituals such as the "ring-shout" emerged as part of slave patterning of common worship. When Martin Luther composed new texts for the congregation to sing, he reshaped antecedent chant melodies into free metrical hymn tunes. The resulting fusion of text and tune introduced a new aesthetic. At the same time, John Calvin allowed only metrical psalm texts to be sung—but, surprisingly, to newly minted tunes derived from French court dances! Ulrich Zwingli found music so emotionally powerful that he silenced instruments and singing, lest worshipers be distracted from the pure Word and grace of God.

Not only are the elements of liturgy just cited "from" particular human arts within particular cultures or sub-cultures, but liturgy is always practiced in the wider domain of social/cultural engagements. There is no "pure" participation in the sense that persons and the means of participation in worship are culture-transcendent. Christian assemblies have always employed "borrowed" materials and artistic means in the worship of God. This does not mean, of course, that there are no culture-transcending forces at work in faithful liturgical celebration. The fifth and sixth theses reintroduce the necessity for culture-critique in the very forms of worship.

Performative Artful Symbolic Action

The second thesis claims that Christian liturgy is an art, but not, in the first instance, a "work of art." In his discussion of what constitutes a "work of art," Nicholas Wolterstorff observes a number of diverse conceptions. A basic definition is that "a work of *fine* art is just that of a product of one of the *fine* arts."[14] But if we want a concept that combines the idea of the aesthetic dimension of human life along with some notion of human intention, we come to define a work of art as " . . . an entity made or presented in order to serve as object of aesthetic contemplation."[15] While there are certainly contemplative dimensions in Christian liturgy (more in some traditions than in others), the point is that the worshipers contemplate God and the divine life, not the liturgy. Or more precisely, it is by means of the liturgy that worshipers contemplate God in certain traditions. Here we need to distinguish "aesthetic" and "religious" contemplation, though the latter characteristically used aesthetic means—at least within so-called kataphatic traditions of devotion and piety. Apophatic traditions aim at the removal of all images and aesthetic means—though often paradoxically with the aid of images in the process of practicing their negation.

In further consideration of how and why liturgy may or may not become an "object" of aesthetic interest and contemplation, the work of Kierkegaard, Edwards, Barth, and von Balthasar become relevant. The question is not either liturgy or aesthetics, either liturgy or the arts, but rather is about the complex relations between the aesthetic and religious forms of participation within particular liturgical traditions.

To confront the problematic status of beauty and aesthetic sensibility in liturgical participation, it is necessary in our present situation to begin with what George Steiner has called our "fragile schooling in humanity."[16] Could one of the distinctive roles of faithful Christian liturgy be to strengthen and deepen this schooling in humanity? What else can the assembly bring and offer to God? Whatever social vision of the good, whatever culture-permeated practices of speaking, singing, beholding, or enacting in concert are employed, these are the defining means of participation. We shall refer to this as the "phenomenal/aesthetic" level of participation in thesis five. Theological claims about the divine/human transaction in worship must attend to the incarnate human means. All too often, theological claims are contravened and subverted by the forms of celebration and the diminished perception of Word and sacrament in actual assemblies. How the phenomenal/aesthetic level is related to the "ecclesial" and "mystical" levels of participation is a key question raised by thesis five.

We cannot now speak so confidently of God in ecclesial life as could be done in earlier times. This is because of the permeability of what is culturally (and theologically) "inside" and "outside" the church. The culture of hype and the banality of evil and of purported human cultural values we desire create a dissonance. Only by moving through the ways in which liturgical elements are subject to both a hermeneutics of cultural appropriation (and appreciation) and a hermeneutics of cultural suspicion can we arrive at the conditions for understanding the relationship of the three primary levels of liturgical participation. Nostalgia for some "pure" liturgy and for some unambiguous "age of faith" may even mislead us concerning the soteriological dimensions of liturgical aesthetics. What can be made clear, however, is my conviction that authentic liturgical participation "in Spirit and in truth" provides a way of living in the face of the harsh ambiguities and the human ambivalence toward the holiness of God's incarnate life in Jesus Christ, suffering, dead, and rising.

Originating in the "Liturgy" of Jesus Christ

Thus thesis three is central to assessments of particular patterns of worship. The Christian assembly originates in narratives and signs gathered about the life, teaching, deeds, suffering, death, and resurrection of Jesus Christ. I refer to this pattern as his "liturgy." Since what he said and did must be enacted together in light of his dying and being raised, the continuing enactment of the saving mystery claimed by Christian faith requires a fusion of verbal and non-verbal modes of life. There are narratives surrounding and leading to and from what he uttered, in both testaments of Scripture. It is helpful to think of the "liturgy" of Jesus as an incarnate enacted parable of God. But the language of the liturgy—in reading, proclamation, prayer, and song—is itself performative, not simply informative.

Texts in Christian liturgy, both written and spoken, are radically dependent for their meaning and point on that which is not language at all. The rhetorical arts in preaching cannot be sustained unless a community also learns to receive and give, to feed and be fed, to wash and be washed, to judge and be judged, to love and be loved, to reconcile and be reconciled, to forgive and be forgiven, and to refer all things to God. In order for what Jesus said and did to be transacted in the present saying and doing of the liturgical action, the pattern of his life is to be received under the signs of his suffering, dying, and rising. Here we also anticipate the eschatological nature of Christian liturgy. The very act of assembling is based on the divine promises to bring to fulfillment that which was spoken by the prophets and which was said and done in Jesus Christ. This leads directly to one of the central proposals of this project: we encounter the most intense unity of his word and deed imaged in the stories and strong symbols of dying and rising in the liturgy of Holy Week, especially in the Triduum and the Easter Vigil. Here the paradoxical tensions lie in wait, so to speak, for the human assembly.

These intensities, I shall argue, are present in various modalities in each Christian assembly. This is not simply a description; it is also a normative claim against the resistances of human cultures.

Permanent Tensions

This takes us into the point of the fifth thesis, returning to the fourth below. The authenticity and relevance of Christian liturgy to any specific cultural context is dependent upon how well (and whether under adequate aesthetic forms) the permanent tensions of the Christian Gospel are shown. We shall note that this "showing" or manifestation in liturgical action requires appropriate "saying" as well. In faithful and authentic Christian liturgy we confront a series of tensions: between the "already and the not-yet" of the kingdom of God, between material form and spiritual substance, between the mediation of the divine in human modalities and the mystery of the divine and the tensions of possible idolatries and deceptions. Because human beings bring existential struggles to liturgical participation, the tension between the "holy" and the "unholy" is always present in some form in every worshiping assembly.

The analysis of distinctive tensions within the proclamation of the Gospel and the central mystery celebrated at the heart of all Christian rites will shed light on the idea of "kenotic aesthetic." Only by viewing Christian liturgy as an eschatological art, with a distinctive kenotic element in its employment of cultural aesthetics, can we begin to reply to the problematic status of worship in contemporary American culture.

Thesis five is an integrating point for the previous four. Borrowing from a classical notion of levels of liturgical participation, I propose that three interrelated levels are required to illuminate the depth and complexity of the divine/human interaction in faithful Christian worship. The first or phenomenal level involves all the "arts" and the attendant "aesthetics" of experience. Here differences across Christian traditions of practice and experience must be taken into account. Each may involve distinctive patterns of perception and styles of participation. Thus the phenomenological task is to render a persuasive account of how singing, praying, listening, gesturing, movement, and ritual engagement entail the use, the

modification, and even the transformation of specific "cultural aesthetics." This requires a thick description of any particular community at worship.

Three Levels of Participation

If we are to speak of Christian liturgy, then the second level,
the level of active/contemplative participation, must be related to
an awareness of ecclesial solidarity. All the "active participation" of
which *Sacrosanctum Concilium* so boldly speaks (and which contemporary Protestant worship admonishes!) may or may not involve
participation as the church—the catholicity of the community gathered about Jesus Christ "in all times and places." Here one of the
distinctive marks of Christian liturgical participation is solidarity
with the living and the dead in Christ, and a notion of conjoining
"earthly worship" with the "worship of heaven."

Arguing from the centrality of the mystery of the incarnate
Christ, suffering, dead, buried, resurrected, and ascended, the third
level of participation engages in the mystery of the divine life itself
in its revealed and revealing form. Here we must be careful to distinguish "mystery" from "mystification." The sense of the co-pres-
ence and even co-inherence of divinity and humanity is part of this
mystery. Without specific occasions focused on the transfiguration
of the human by virtue of the paschal mystery, we cannot fully discern the way in which the aesthetic and the ecclesial levels are con-
summated in the "participation in the life of God." Lacking this,
Christian public worship cannot fully achieve its own self-critique,
nor can it hope to address the resistances of contemporary American culture. I propose that lacking a sense of the interrelated character of these levels of liturgical participation, Christian liturgy cannot "show" its capacity for "culture-transcendence." This is necessary to determine whether or not we can speak of the paradox of
employed culturally specific "aesthetics" in order to offer a theological critique of the reigning cultural aesthetic.

Specific examples from so-called "traditional" and "contemporary" worship forms and patterns show how it is possible to develop
a sense for the phenomenal/aesthetic level without receptivity to
the ecclesial; or how both of these may be present, but not related to

the eschatological dimensions of the mystery of the divine glory. This approach sheds light on a theological retrieval of the relations between beauty and holiness.

While my investigation begins with the most obvious sense of participation in and through aesthetic (artistic) means, it also seeks to uncover the linkages between all three levels of participation. We can honor the *Constitution on the Sacred Liturgy* in calling for "full, conscious, and active participation" of the faithful. At the same time, this can be deceiving if we think that is sufficient, or that it can simply be brought about by pragmatic or instrumentalist techniques. Rather, the question of the aesthetic criteria guiding "full, active, and conscious" must be embedded in theological claims attendant upon being the Body of Christ at worship. This, as I have already suggested requires a palpable sense of catholicity. But even more crucial is the reality of belonging to the community marked by the dying and rising Christ. These, too, imply and require aesthetic embodiment. These we find supremely in the pattern and content of the Easter Triduum. While always enacted in particular times and cultural settings, the dynamics of the central mystery of Christian faith holds the key to issues of "culture transcendence."

Here the paradox of the kenotic Christ suggests what Joseph Gelineau called the "paschal human in Christ" as a norm of judgment on all cultural aesthetic powers. This norm is simultaneously a hermeneutics of appreciation and a hermeneutics of suspicion. The capacities to reflect the glory of God in and through music, the visual, the kinetic, and the ritually symbolic belong to each specific culture; yet the presumptive and ambivalent character of those same cultures stand under the judgment. Each particular culture has a range of aesthetic means and a range of aesthetic sensibilities. Some, like so-called "traditional cultures," may certainly have a more uniform set of means and sensibility. By contrast, the characteristic attributed to "post-modern" cultures is one of fragmented strands and a splintering into "sub-cultures" with little in common. My argument is not dependent upon opposing traditional or "classical" to contemporary or "post-modern" cultures. The key point is that each culture, however circumscribed, must bring its own aesthetic means and sensibility to Christian liturgy in order to understand what must be "broken" and judged by the central symbols of the Christian faith.

If Christian faith and thought continually orient and re-orient around the saving mystery of the life, teaching, death, and resurrection of Jesus Christ, then the continuing enactment of that mystery in word and ritual action (the living utterance, the meal, and the water bath) both requires and continually judges the aesthetics brought to liturgy. The arts brought to the liturgical assembly are necessary and must be assessed not on purely aesthetic grounds, as with "works of art." Instead, they are to be held as subject to the inner paradox that Christian liturgy celebrates: the kenotic aesthetic found in Christ. This sensibility and perceptive capability is encountered and formed in human communities who stand under the "glory of the cross." This itself is a peculiar disposition, not simply given in the natural inclinations of the human spirit. It is received. Like the virtue of humility, it is a strong receptivity, a vulnerability to that which is other than our own self-ideals.

The tensive character of faithful liturgical aesthetics issues in both a way of perceiving, and a way of being, in the world. The world is beheld "as" a created order. The world is seen "as" the arena of God's concern and activity. The words of Scripture are heard "as" an address to us. This "seeing as" and "hearing as" is part of the imaginative re-orientation to life and to the whole cosmos that vital and authentic liturgy provides. This is often precisely because the surrounding culture resists it. Such a vision and a way of life is therefore not a product of human artistry, much less an "experience" of the aesthetic kind. Rather, only by deploying the central symbols and stories of the Christian Gospel with aesthetic power in light of the kenotic life of God in Christ are such a vision and way of life possible.

"Work and culture are the place where human beings and the world meet in the glory of God."[17] But Jean Corbon speaks of how this is obscured and resisted by human beings who lack a sense of divine glory. "If the universe is to be recognized and experienced," he claims, "as filled with [God's] glory, human beings must first become once again the dwelling places of this glory and be clothed in it; . . . ."[18] This, I will argue, is only possible because of the self-emptying of all pretense to divinity. This is the means of grace at the heart of the passion narrative of Christ, and of the passion of God to save God's people, and indeed, all creation.

The aesthetics of Christian liturgy cannot therefore be confined to considerations of beauty and sensibility, though it requires these. The coming to see and to live in the world "as" God's good creation, fallen and redeemed by divine grace in actual time and history, is also a coming to envision the good, and to be drawn to do it. This is not to be an "aesthetic experience" in the liturgy (though this may, from time to time, occur), but a being formed in the affections and dispositions to live out in the "liturgy of life" the paradoxical beauty beheld in the paschal human freely offered.

Communion with God is part of the ground and the *telos* of authentic and faithful liturgy. But the beauty of this communion is held captive in the forces of every culture. This is, in part, what is meant by sin. The eschatological vision offered at the heart of Christian worship is found in what God glories in. As St. Ireneaus claimed, "The glory of God is living human beings, and the life of human beings is the vision of God . . . for the glory of human beings is God, but the receptacle of the Energy of God and of his entire Wisdom and his entire Power is human beings."[19]

Liturgy as Eschatological Art in Action

This brings us to the threshold of the eschatological character of every Christian assembly. Participation in the divine life requires making visible, audible, and palpable the vision of the good for all creation. The "glory" of God is thus not simply in creation, or in human artistry, but is found most powerfully in the face of the dying and risen Christ, and is promised in the vision of God's Shalom for all creation, for "heaven and earth." Christian liturgy that obscures, or fails to bring a maturation into, the mystery of God's glory and promises for the world, falls prey to cultural and "aesthetic" captivities of every kind.

Chief among the cultural captivities is the tyranny of the "immediate" of "hype," and especially of the banality of violence present in North American electronic entertainment culture. Only by sustained practices of holding the human before an alternative image of the human before God can these captivities be addressed. If my synoptic exposition and analysis of the intrinsic aesthetic dimensions of Christian liturgy are at all near the mark, then a sketch of a liturgical critique of culture is possible. Barth and von Balthasar can join van der Leeuw at this point: "the doctrine of the image of God includes an entire theological aesthetics or aesthetical theology. In the form of the crucified, humiliated, and problematic, yet eternally worthy of worship, lies a judgment, but at the same time also a justification, for all human attempts at creating form."[20] More significantly, the restored and eschatologically oriented *imago dei* is offered at the heart of Christian liturgical life over time, in every cultural context.

For all this, a fundamental problem remains. Human beings live simultaneously in several "cultural worlds." These are not consistent or even congruent with one another. "Post-modernity" is a phrase used to name this reality. Whether the kenotic aesthetic of Christian liturgy, and its attendant "paschal human" iconography for culture, can reach into these other social/cultural inhabitations is not something a specific "liturgical theology" or particular aesthetic approach to liturgical celebrations can guarantee. The cultural-transcendent aspects of liturgical life are not manipulable by human artistic means. But what is possible is continual attentiveness to the qualities in liturgical participation that set conditions for the Holy Spirit to yet transfigure and transform our cultural captivities. Such attentiveness is itself a profoundly aesthetic matter. The "ritual logic of Christian public prayer and sacrament is primarily embodied and sensory, imagistic, and experiential, rather than cognitive or intellectual."[21]

In our present North American entertainment culture, Christian liturgy must cultivate those symbolic means that can evoke, sustain, and empower a vision of God and of the cosmos in which beauty and goodness coinhere in life, not simply in thought or in individual personal experience. The assessment of ritual practices—with, in, and through their diverse aesthetic forms—requires continual testing for adequacy to self-giving glory of the divine life poured out into the whole creation, in light of the passion and cross. This we recognize as holy—awesomely and sublimely beyond our rational grasp, hinted at and evoked by symbolic, metaphorical, and parabolic participation. For human beings and human societies, the tensive holding together of what is not holy with the holy is practiced in the liturgy.[22] There, we may say—but without presumption— it is effected and brought to life.

Embracing the Tensions: Active Receptivity

The active receptivity toward beauty and holiness must itself learn the permanent tensions in the worship of God. Whatever the beauty of God is, for the Christian worshiping assembly, it must include the brokenness and the non-beauty of the crucifixion. This is the extreme point of tension. Thus we encounter the two primary causes for theological suspicion of the discourse of beauty: idolatry and distraction.

Because Christian worship, in nearly all its manifestations, employs a range of artistic means, the church must always be in the midst of sorting out the immediately attractive from the culturally durable. A proper ambivalence toward the aesthetics of worship is thus a virtue. Faithfulness and relevance of Christian liturgy in our present cultural context is dependent upon how well these permanent tensions of Christian faith are offered, experienced, and reflected upon. We are confronted with a series of tensions *intrinsic* to the act of worship itself: between the "already" and the "not yet" of the kingdom of God; between the material forms and the spiritual substance of the various arts we employ; between the "hearing" and the "coming-to-see"; between participating in liturgy and living faithful lives toward the good in the midst of moral and ethical struggles; between true and false prophesy, between holiness and all the idolatries of which we are capable. The aesthetics of Christian liturgy serve also as an act of resistance against societal forces and structures that lead to human self-deception and dullness to whatever is true, lovely, and of good report. Active receptivity toward the kenosis of incarnate deity is both the means and the goal of faithful liturgical life.

Endnotes

1. Gerardus van der Leeuw, *Sacred and Profane Beauty: The Holy in Art*, trans. David E. Green (New York: Holt, Reinhart and Winston, 1963), 110.

2. Albert Rouet observes that "if the Church has been and remains suspicious of the body, this is because the body offers the prime temptation toward self-absorption and becomes the principal means for captivating others. [This] real danger shows, however, that the occasion for the risk is equally an occasion for transfiguration." Albert Rouet, *Liturgy and the Arts*, trans. Paul Philibert, O.P. (Collegeville: The Liturgical Press, 1997), 148-149.

3. David N. Power, *Unsearchable Riches: The Symbolic Nature of Liturgy* (New York: Pueblo Publishing Co., 1984), 74.

4. Hans Urs von Balthasar, *The Glory of the Lord: A Theological Aesthetics*, Vol. I: *Seeing the Form*, trans. Erasmo Leiva-Merikakis (San Francisco: Ignatius Press, 1982), 19.

5. *Ibid.*, 23

6. This does not mean that considerations of taste are irrelevant. Frank Burch Brown has written convincingly about relations between taste and religious imagination in worship and spirituality. See his *Good Taste, Bad Taste, and Christian Taste: Aesthetics in Religious Life* (New York: Oxford University Press, 2000) especially 3-25.

7. Romano Guardini, *The Spirit of the Liturgy*, trans. Ada Lane (New York: Crossroad Publishers, 1988).

8. I will return to this in the sixth thesis explored in the next section of the essay. For an earlier extensive exposition of the idea of eschatological art, see Don E. Saliers, *Worship As Theology: Foretaste of Glory Divine* (Nashville: Abingdon Press, 1994).

9. I am indebted to the work of Gordon W. Lathrop for the methodological significance of "juxtaposition." He presents a persuasive account of how the generative tensions (the old and the new, type and anti-type, word and symbol) within Scripture carry over into Christian worship. See *Holy Things: A Liturgical Theology* (Minneapolis: Fortress Press, 1995).

10. *The Confessions of St. Augustine*, Book X, 6.

11. Karl Barth, *Church Dogmatics II/1*, trans. G. W. Bromiley (Edinburgh: T. & T. Clark, 1961), 650.

12. Aidan Kavanagh, "The Politics of Symbol and Art," *Symbol and Art in Worship*, ed. Luis Maldonado and David Power, *Concilium: Religion in the Eighties*, No. 132 (Edinburgh: T. & T. Clark; New York: Seabury Press, 1980), 38.

13. James F. White, *Introduction to Christian Worship*, 2nd ed. (Nashville: Abingdon Press, 1997), chapter one.

14. Nicholas Wolterstorff, *Art In Action: Toward A Christian Aesthetic* (Grand Rapids: Wm. B. Eerdmanns, 1980), 17. The italics are his.

15. *Ibid.*, 18.

16. George Steiner, *Real Presences* (Chicago: University of Chicago Press, 1989), 193.

17. Jean Corbon, *The Wellspring of Worship*, trans. Matthew J. O'Connell (New York/Mahwah: Paulist Press, 1988), 158. These comments are in the context of his discussion of the Orthodox conception of "divinization" of the human person. "If our gaze is to liberate the beauty hidden in all things, it must first be bathed with light in him whose gaze sends beauty streaming out." 162.

18. *Ibid.*, 158.

19. Irenaeus, *Against the Heresies* IV, 20, 7: III, 20,2, translation found in Jean Corbon, *op. cit.*, 200.

20. Gerardus van der Leeuw, *Sacred and Profane Beauty: The Holy in Art, op. cit.*, 327.

21. Nathan D. Mitchell, *Liturgy and the Social Sciences* (Collegeville: The Liturgical Press, 1999), 6.

22. This theme is carried out persuasively in Gordon W. Lathrop's work. See *Holy Things: A Liturgical Theology* (Minneapolis: Fortress Press, 1995) and *Holy People: A Liturgical Ecclesiology* (Minneapolis: Fortress Press, 1999).

"Are You Alone Wise?"
Debates about Certainty in
Early Modernity

Susan E. Schreiner
UNIVERSITY OF CHICAGO DIVINITY SCHOOL
CHICAGO, ILLINOIS

Early modernity was a time of great changes, including the collapse of older ways of thinking, the breaking up of Western Christendom, the tumult in traditional (and supposedly eternal) institutions, the rapid increase in knowledge, and the waging of religious wars. Thinkers of both the sixteenth and the early seventeenth centuries experienced their ages as unsettling and disorienting. Stephen Greenblatt astutely depicts this sense of disorientation as a feeling of "great unmooring," the sense that "fixed positions have become unstuck," and the anxious awareness that the moral landscape was shifting. Religious polemicists demonstrated how "each other's religion—the very anchor of millions of souls— was a cunning theatrical illusion, a demonic fantasy and a piece of poetry." It was a time, Greenblatt concludes, when "truth itself was radically unstable."[1]

The changes that swept through Europe causing this sense of disorientation made this era preoccupied with the search for certainty. This preoccupation dominated the terms and conclusions of nearly all topics and debates. The overt theological and philosophical debates of early modernity were those of epistemology, justification, ecclesiology, and the sacraments. Underlying these issues were broader problems regarding the crisis of authority, the search for salvation, and the hermeneutical dilemmas in biblical interpretation. When we look closely we discover that the concepts, vocabulary, arguments, and presuppositions of all these controversies were expressed in terms of the overarching problem of certitude which permeated the entire age. Armed with the question of certainty, the historian can examine almost any subject: the Hussites, the Catholic polemicists, the Scripture principle, the Radical Reformers, the theologies of justification, the ecclesiological and sacramental debates, and the rise of scepticism. Nearly every major thinker of the era demonstrates this concern with certitude and fear of deception and error: Luther, Zwingli, Calvin, Thomas More, Cajetan, Johann Eck, Las Casas, Bruno, Cervantes, Thomas Münzter, Hans Denck, Sebastian Franck, Castellio, Carlstadt, the *Beneficio di Cristo*, the Council of Trent, Teresa of Avila, Montaigne, and Shakespeare. This essay cannot consider all of these thinkers. Therefore, I have concentrated primarily on limited discussions with a sampling of examples primarily by Luther, Thomas More, Montaigne, and Shakespeare.

To state my thesis much too broadly and briefly, sixteenth-century theologians offered competing forms of certainty. The "magisterial" reformers expounded a doctrine of justification that promised the subjective certitude of salvation. Catholic opponents countered with a certainty based on visible authority; that is, the authority of the ancient, divinely ordained, hierarchical and *knowable* church. Despite their differences, both sides claimed the Spirit as the agent of certainty. Catholics argued that unless one could know with certitude *where* the Spirit is, no one could claim any knowledge of salvific truth. According to the Catholic position, the Spirit was inseparable from the church, a church that the Spirit had guided for centuries. The emergence of religious radicalism and the ongoing sacramental controversies made the Protestant appeal to the Spirit very problematic. In response to these opponents, the magisterial reformers appealed to the Spirit in order to justify their claim to the certainty of salvation as well as to authorize their biblical interpretation.

The Certitude of Salvation and Authority

The problem of certainty first fully emerged in the sixteenth century with regard to the problem of justification. Medieval Catholic doctrines of justification had always denied the subjective, individual certitude of salvation. The believer could have "objective" certainty that the elect would be saved and "conjectural" certainty that one has certain signs that he or she might be saved. But the need for complete holiness meant that as long as sin remained, the *viator* could not be so rash or prideful as to suppose that he was saved. The Tridentine fathers confirmed this view in 1547 when they condemned the "vain and ungodly confidence" of heretics who boasted about their subjective certainty of salvation. According to Trent, when the Christian considers his own sinfulness he may quite appropriately have a pious fear "concerning his own grace since no one can know with the certainty of faith, which cannot err, that he has obtained the grace of God."[2] Sixteenth-century Catholicism upheld the medieval assumption that the need for holiness and the desire for subjective certitude of salvation canceled each other out.

The novelty of Luther's doctrine lay both in his rejection of the need for holiness and in his redefinition of faith as certainty. Whereas Trent saw confidence as "ungodly," Luther viewed *fiducia* as the radical trust in the promise of salvation by faith alone. Luther's doctrine of justification provided for the subjective certitude of salvation precisely because it replaced holiness with a new conception of saving faith. In place of a faith "working through love," Luther spoke of a faith that bore within its very nature the experiential, individual certainty of salvation. The faith that justified was not a faith formed by love but, to borrow medieval terminology, a faith formed by certitude. To talk explicitly about salvation, Luther most frequently referred to the inner certainty of being in a state of grace. However, John 6:44 and John 14:9 propelled Luther to go further and to affirm the certitude of election. Commenting on Genesis 26:9, Luther stated that Christ "came into the world to make us certain" and that God revealed himself so that "you may know whether you are predestined or not."[3] The centrality of his concern with certainty is clearest in his 1535 exegesis of Galatians 4:6 ("God has sent the Spirit of his Son into your hearts crying, 'Abba Father!')." Since believers have the "Spirit of adoption," they should

> Strive daily to move more and more from uncertainty to certainty . . . for if we are in doubt about our being in a state of grace and about our being pleasing to God, we are denying that Christ has redeemed us . . . Let us thank God that we have been delivered from this monster of uncertainty and that now we can believe with certainty that the Holy Spirit is crying and issuing a sigh too deep for words in our hearts . . . Now that the plague of uncertainty, with which the entire church of the pope is infected, is driven away, let us believe with certainty that God is favorably disposed toward us . . . [4]

The claim for the subjective certitude of salvation was reaffirmed by both Zwingli and Calvin. Unlike Luther, Zwingli was only too happy to discuss predestination. Indeed his defense of certitude had its origin in his doctrine of God's immutable election. He differed from Luther primarily because of his insistence that one finds certainty by contemplating election directly. The key to Zwingli's belief in the certitude of faith was his teaching that election preceded faith. Using John 6:44, Zwingli affirmed that faith is not within human power. As Galatians 5:22 proved, the very existence of faith was due to the inner presence of the divine Spirit. Reasoning backwards, Zwingli argued that "faith is the sign of election" and that "faith is given to those who have been elected and ordained to eternal life but in such a way that election precedes faith and faith follows election." Zwingli could then conclude that the experience of faith in itself is proof of the certainty of salvation: "Be assured that he who believes has been elected by the Father and predestined and called. He believes, therefore, because he has been elected and predestined to eternal salvation."[5]

The doctrine of the certainty of faith recurred in Calvin. Opposing medieval distinctions between types of faith, Calvin wrote that, "Now we shall possess a right definition of faith if we call it a firm and certain knowledge of God's benevolence toward us, founded upon the truth of the freely given promise in Christ, both revealed to our minds and sealed upon our hearts through the Holy Spirit."[6] For Calvin, faith effects an experiential certitude of salvation, a boldness and confidence of spiritual adoption. Therefore he concluded that "faith is not content with an obscure and confused conception; but requires full and fixed certainty such . . . as things experienced and proved."[7]

These depictions of faith as certainty demonstrate the frequent and growing use of experiential and affective language among the reformers. Luther repeatedly spoke of an "inner assurance," a "tasting," "feeling," "sweetening," and "experiencing" of the inner certainty within the "heart" of the believer. Zwingli attributed this inward feeling of certitude to the immediacy between the divine and human spirit. According to Zwingli, the "Spirit binds our soul to himself. . . and he who has not this certainty so that he feels it stand forth in the veins of his soul should pray daily, 'Lord, increase our faith.'"[8] Calvin also employed this affective vocabulary. With his insistence that faith pertains to both mind and heart, Calvin used this affective language to describe the experiential reality of certitude. "Uneasy doubting" is replaced by the "feeling of full assurance," which cannot occur "without our truly feeling its sweetness and experiencing it in ourselves."[9] Romans 1:17 is commonly considered the most important verse for Reformation theology. Equally crucial, however, for all the reformers was Galatians 4:6; the cry of "Abba Father!" was possible only for those who no longer saw God as a judge but who "experienced" God as a "Father." Thus Galatians 4:6 could be uttered only by believers who "tasted" and "felt" the "Spirit of adoption" within the soul.[10]

If this affective language had remained limited to issues of justification, subsequent debates about authority might not have taken the problematic turn that came to characterize sixteenth-century polemics. However, as the affective language about the certainty of salvation was transferred quickly to the realm of authority, reformation arguments followed an important but disturbing trajectory. Clearly the difficulty was how to adjudicate experience. An impasse emerged because of the constant appeal to the Spirit as the giver of this inner experience of certainty. The internal testimony of the Holy Spirit became the common foundation on which all opponents based their certitude of authority. The most serious example of this impasse was the eruption of the sacramental and spiritualist controversies. In these debates, opposing parties claimed that inner *testimonium* or *illuminatio,* which authorized their theological positions and, most importantly, their own biblical interpretations.

Fundamentally the magisterial reformers argued for the material sufficiency of Scripture as interpreted within the church and with the aid of the exegetical tradition. This sufficiency of Scripture was based on the belief that the Bible could be the reliable authority in theological disputes because its "literal" sense was clear.[11] Later debates about Eucharistic and baptismal texts severely tested this principle. Known by scholars for the differing views on the relation between sign and thing signified, these debates also pointed to a deeper underlying crisis of authority for the reformers. The sacramental controversies actually ended the "exegetical optimism" of the Reformation and raised the inevitable suspicion that this form of "biblicism" was a perilous replacement for the papacy as the ultimate source of authority.[12] Opposing parties were reading the same passages with critically different interpretations. The sacramental debates went beyond the specific theological principles under discussion. Ultimately these controversies intensified the more essential overarching problem of the authority to interpret Scripture.

A hermeneutical crisis of authority had arisen, a crisis that was answered increasingly by the all too familiar claim to the Spirit. Now *both* the text of Scripture and the experience of the Spirit guaranteed the certainty of one's exegesis. Nor was the claim to the Spirit limited to the Spiritualist radicals. Luther valiantly defended himself against the charge of subjectivism and individualism. He made clear that the principle of *sola Scriptura* was never intended to mean that the Bible should be interpreted individually apart from the hermeneutical tradition, the councils, and the testimony of the Fathers. Moreover, as Oberman has demonstrated, Luther argued in response to the radicals that the hermeneutical principle lies not in the reader but in Scripture itself. Yet Scripture must be based on Christ as the "Master Builder," a reality that is handed down by the visible church. Hence Luther could write, "It [the Christian church] is the Mother that begets and bears every Christian through the Word of God . . . ; where Christ is not preached, there is no Holy Spirit to create, call, and gather the Christian Church, and outside of it no one can come to the Lord Christ."[13] Nonetheless, this attempt to guard against subjectivism depended on Luther's debatable conviction that he knew exactly where the "Christian Church" existed in the sixteenth century. Luther's opponents concentrated always on the alleged "spiritualism" found in Luther's writings, particularly his earlier treatises. To some extent they were quite justified. As George Williams observed, "the vagaries [about the relationship between Word and Spirit] should not obscure from view that a large element in the spiritualism of the Radical Reformation goes back to Luther himself and, to a lesser extent, Zwingli."[14]

In some respects Luther gave his critics plenty of ammunition. His difficult concept of *sola Scriptura* was often explained in terms of both anthropology and pneumatology. He vehemently maintained that the severity of the noetic effect of sin requires that human reason be redeemed and illumined before it can understand the Word. Thus in arguing that Scripture is "clear" he also taught the necessity for the inner illumination of the Spirit for understanding the biblical text. Word and Spirit are inseparable in such a way that the fallen mind can perceive the clear and true meaning of Scripture only when inwardly inspired by the Spirit. This "spiritualist" element, is seen most dramatically in the frequent use by Luther (and Zwingli) of 1 Cor. 2:15, "The spiritual man judges all things."[15] The inner illumination of the Spirit justified the exclusivity of one's scriptural interpretation as well as the authority to judge as heretical the interpretation of one's opponents.

The Emergence of Religious Radicalism

Luther's attempt to forestall any charge of individualism was in response to his Catholic opponents and, increasingly, to the growing presence of religious radicalism. In the years that followed Luther's break with Rome, men such as Müntzer, Carlstadt, Denck, and Franck all appealed to an immediate, affective, inner experience that authorized their action and exegesis.[16] These dissenters argued that Scripture gave only a witness but not the "experience" of faith. Only an "experienced faith" instilled by the Spirit could establish the right to preach the Word authoritatively. For Müntzer, only the experience of a faith tested by suffering and given by the Spirit gave the ability to interpret Scripture:

> Through experiencing unbelief the elect leaves behind him all the counterfeit faith he has learnt, heard, or read from Scripture; for he sees that an outward testimony cannot create inward reality . . . Hence he is not deflected by anything said by those lacking in experience . . .
>
> The scholar cannot grasp the meaning of Scripture, although the whole of it has been expounded to him in a human way, and although he may be about to burst apart [with all his knowledge]; he has to wait until the key of David has revealed it to him . . .Then man will be taught by God alone, person to person, and not by a created being."[17]

Although with differing theologies, other radical dissenters echoed this reliance on "experienced faith" granted by the Spirit to the elect. Denck argued that "Scripture is not its own interpreter, but rather interpretation belongs to the Holy Spirit who first gave Scripture. One must have the interpretation of the Spirit before one can be certain. Where this interpretation is not present, what one knows is false and nothing."[18] For Denck, the authority of Scripture itself was contingent upon its confirmation and clarification of that which is experienced inwardly.[19] Carlstadt reiterated these sentiments saying that "As far as I am concerned I do not need the outward witness. I want to have the testimony of the Spirit within me. . . . This is how it was with the apostles who were assured inwardly by the testimony of the Spirit and later preached Christ outwardly."[20] The priority of the inward and experiential over the external also found expression in Franck who insisted that faith must be "received in experience." He concluded that "the inner man believes only what he has learned, heard, seen, and experienced by God . . . therefore, experience is like a key to Scripture."[21]

The Certitude of Authority

With all these competing claims to the authority of spiritual illumination, the problem quickly became, "Where is the Spirit?" Catholic opponents answered by offering a powerful competing certitude but not one based on the certainty of salvation or the experiential illumination of the Spirit. Spotting a difficulty in appealing to the certainty offered by spiritual illumination, Catholic polemicists brought to bear against the reformers the weight of history and tradition. Perceiving a difficulty with Luther's statements on authority, they asked if the true church could exist in one poor monk who defied the universal church. Luther's bravado was shaken by the mocking question, "Are you alone wise?. . .You [Luther] are not the only one who has Scripture and God's word. . . . Do we not have the Spirit just as you do? Are so many others mistaken? Suppose you are wrong and thus drag so many with you into eternal damnation?"[22] This jeer so haunted Luther that he insisted it was really the devil who was taunting him with this question. That "devil" may have been no other than his archenemy Johann Eck:

> If the whole Scripture is so completely clear, it is a wonder that the Holy Fathers, who read it so frequently, did not understand it for 1,200 years. If it was obscure to Augustine, Jerome, Bernard, and Thomas, how will it be clear to Lutheran laymen?[23]

The same argument was vehemently taken up by Thomas More:

> For you are accustomed to boast that you are certain
> that you have your teaching from heaven; spiritual
> man that you are. . . . If you argue that God is
> indicating to you at the present time so many, such
> useful, such necessary truths, why should you think
> that he concealed all these truths for such a long
> time from such holy men to the great detriment of
> His whole church? But he did not conceal them,
> Luther. Rather, God opened their eyes and
> responded to their humility, whereas, rejecting your
> arrogance, he allows you to appear wise in your own
> eyes.[24]

In opposition to the divisions within Protestantism, Eck and
More posed the universal, monolithic and ancient church of Catholicism. The disputed verse became John 16:13: "When the Spirit of
truth comes, he will guide you into all truth." Both Eck and More
insisted that the Spirit is indeed the giver of certitude but is promised only to the church, not to specific individuals. Truth resides in
the "unity of the Spirit" preserved throughout history in the divinely
ordained, hierarchical, and *knowable* Catholic church. The church
cannot err in matters essential to salvation because she always has
had Christ as the bridegroom and because "she is ruled by the teaching authority of the Holy Spirit who has never abandoned her."[25]
The issue of authority is clearly prominent in these sixteenth-century polemics. The Catholic position on authority is misunderstood
if it is seen only as a fear of social anarchy or as a means to crush
the Reformation by an oppressive authoritarianism. In the Catholic argument authority became an alternative form of certainty. The
power of the appeals to authority by Eck and More is that instead of
joining pneumatology with the Word and experience, they joined
pneumatology with ecclesiology. In so doing they succeeded in link-
ing ecclesiology to certitude. In their view one must begin with a
true ecclesiology in order to know with certainty where the "Spirit
of Truth" could be found.

In order to make ecclesiology a promise of certitude, Catholic
polemicists maintained that one has to know *where* the true church
can be found. With this argument, Eck and More touched on a problem that recurred in the theologies of the reformers, particularly
those of Luther, Zwingli, and many of the Spiritualists. The issue

was that of the relationship between hiddenness and clarity, visibility and invisibility. The theologies of hiddenness that so profoundly permeated the thought of the Reformation became for Catholic controversialists an issue of authority. According to the Catholic argument, there can be no certainty without knowability. But there can be no knowability without clear visibility. Ignoring many of Luther's attempts to root the church in the visible signs of baptism, the Eucharist, and preaching, Catholic polemicists argued that in order to offer certainty the church must be clearly or visibly knowable and identifiable. Consequently, More attacked Luther for holding to a church of "Platonic Ideas," which is both "in some place and no place." The church, More insisted, must be "palpable and perceptible." Later More repeated this charge, saying that Tyndale:

> hath in a long processe labored to proue you that
> the chyrch of Cryste is a nother company then the
> knowen catholyke company of all chrysten regyons/
> that is to wytte a certayne secrete scatered
> congregacyon vnknowen to all the worlde besyde,
> and to theyr owne felowes to/ and euery man by hys
> inwarde felynge not onely knowen onely to hym
> selfe, but also so well and surely knowen vnto hym
> selfe for a vertuouse good and faythefull fynall electe
> of god, that he is in hym self very certayne and sure
> that he can not be but saued/ and that he so hath
> the spyryte of god imprysoned in hys breste and so
> faste fetered in hys holy harte. . .[26]

In this passage More clearly identified what he considered the reformers' connection between invisibility, interior certainty, the appeal to the Spirit, and the spiritually authorized claim to authority. The result, he warned, was a church "unknowen to all." Such a church could never be a source for the certitude of truth. For these Catholic thinkers, the identification of visibility and certainty meant that the certitude of the universal church is clearly and visibly known in the councils, the apostolic see, and the ecclesiastical hierarchy. Furthermore, the unity of the church was itself a sign of her knowable, visible, and authoritative certainty.[27] Drawing on Tertullian, Eck maintained that one must belong to the true and knowable church in order to find the correct interpretation of Scripture. Attacking the false authority of "private judgment," Eck insisted that "it must be believed that God inspires a true understanding of Scripture to the. . . unity of the Church rather than to one private man such as Luther, Zwingli, or Osiander."[28] The "Creed of the Council of Trent" (1564), clearly reaffirmed this ecclesiology by stating that private judgment must submit to the "unanimous agreement of the Fathers" and the supremacy of the teaching authority of Rome.[29] At Trent there was an encapsulation of the sixteenth-century Catholic position of figures such as Eck, More, and their fellow controversialists: a denial of the subjective certitude of salvation aligned with a correspondingly high doctrine of the certitude of authority. This doctrine functioned on many levels, the most important of which was to guarantee the knowability, accessibility, and certainty of truth.

The Rise of Skepticism

Claims to certainty continued to divide churches throughout the sixteenth century. Darker forces were also at work. The underside of certainty was the fear of deception and the use of violence toward outsiders. These forces were fueled by the joining of error and deception to the demonic. This connection between deception and the demonic surfaced on all sides of the sixteenth-century religious controversies. Whether one looks at Luther, Carlstadt, More, or Teresa of Avila, the reason for error and doubt was the deception of the devil.[30] Therefore, just as the Spirit was the agent of certainty, Satan became an agent of deception. Furthermore, demonic forces had to be eradicated to ensure the safety of the "true church." From the drowning of the Anabaptists to the work of the Spanish Inquisition, all parties were vigilantly determined to destroy the deceptions of Satan. In the midst of these darker forces, a small but important minority radically questioned the claim to certainty. In fact, the appeal to *uncertainty* first arose in the context of the death penalty for heretics.

The leaders in Geneva inherited the potentially deadly connection between ecclesiology and soteriology and affirmed that the secular power should safeguard the eternal welfare of its citizens. The most famous heresy trial was that of Servetus who, on October 26, 1553, was found guilty of Anabaptism and antitrinitarianism. In accord with the revived code of Justinian, he was executed the following day. Although the condemnation of Servetus had been approved by the Protestant canons, there was an immediate outcry against his execution by more radical dissenters. The most prominent was Castellio who exemplified the voice of caution and restraint.[31] Castellio's writings demonstrate a recoiling from certitude in order to justify a tolerance based on the willingness to live with uncertainty.

Several of Castellio's arguments were traditional; namely, that the conscience could not be coerced and that there must be a distinction between spiritual and temporal powers.[32] But he added a new argument symptomatic of the sixteenth-century preoccupation with certitude. Castellio warned against the dangerous delusion of certainty. His moderate skepticism was not epistemological; he was not primarily interested in the weakness of reason, in the noetic fall or in the essential unknowability of objects. Castellio was concerned with the *danger* posed by certitude.

Castellio's thought was based on a unique combination of ideas; that is, the elevation of human reason coupled with the limitations of human knowledge. Against Calvin, Castellio denied the radical noetic fall. The senses and the intellect were created by God and remain valid instruments to explore, find, and interpret truth. Indeed reason is the "daughter of God."[33] In fact, Castellio replaced the inseparability of Word and Spirit with the rule of reason as the source of authority. But he did so by limiting what reason could know in theological matters. Scripture alone, he argued, was a dangerous basis for authority because it was often unclear. In Scripture there were "enigmas and inscrutable questions" that had been in dispute for centuries. And yet, "for this cause the earth is filled with innocent blood."[34] Reason must know its limits and learn the "art of doubting,"[35] an art that revealed the dangers of certainty on matters beyond the reach of reason. Human beings could not know perfectly who were the true heretics and reason stepped beyond its bounds in trying to judge heresy.[36] In his warnings against a spiritually instilled certainty, Castellio urged believers to be willing to live with uncertainty. In the rush for certitude, he insisted, the essential unknowability of many divine subjects had been denied with disastrous results.

> All sects hold their religion as established by the
> Word of God and call it certain. Therefore all sects
> are armed by Calvin's rule for mutual persecution.
> Calvin says that he is certain, and they say the same.
> He says they are mistaken, and they say the same
> of him. Calvin wishes to be judge and so do they.
> Who will be judge? Why make Calvin the judge of
> all the sects, that he alone should kill? How can he
> prove that he alone knows? He has the Word of God,
> and so do they. If the matter is so certain, to whom
> is it certain?[37]

Rather than claiming certainty, *safety* laid in the recognition of the
limitations of human knowledge. A recognition of this limitation is
the true art of doubting.

> First we must know what matters are to be doubted
> and what is to be known without doubt; further,
> what matters, I will not say ought to remain
> unknown, but may remain unknown and are not
> essential, whereas others can and ought to be known.
> These questions must all be answered.[38]

Castellio actually reiterated several of the arguments made by
Johann Eck and Thomas More. Scripture was indeed unclear about
many matters and we cannot find a final judge by depending only
on the biblical text. Nevertheless, instead of turning to the certitude of authority, Castellio asserted the necessity for *uncertainty*.
He concluded by warning that those "who are unwilling to doubt
anything are rash and dangerous." Only the "art of doubting" could
lead to peace and toleration. Neither the Spirit nor the authority of
the church was the answer for Castellio. The willingness to admit
uncertainty and doubt would alone prevent persecution. The danger of the human desire and claim for certainty had now been
sounded.

Two other voices of the late sixteenth and early seventeenth
centuries also demonstrated the growing awareness of the inevitable uncertainty of human life. Montaigne, an exponent of the new
Pyrrhonism, echoed many of Castellio's themes but in a more radical way. Throughout the *Essays*, and especially in "The Apology for
Raymond Sebond," Montaigne warned the reader to "stay within
his own rank" by recognizing the extreme limits of human knowledge. For Montaigne neither experience nor reason, including the

experience demonstrated by history, could give the mind access to universal truth or certainty. Rather, they gave access only to flux, change, dissolution, variability, and uncertainty:

> There is no permanent existence either in our being or in that of objects. We ourselves, our faculty of judgment and all mortal things are flowing and rolling ceaselessly; nothing certain can be established about one from the other, since both judged and judging are ever shifting and changing.[39]

Montaigne accepted the truth of his Catholic religion because to change or reject Catholicism was an assertion of certainty he could not make. Like the ancient sceptics he advocated a conservative life in harmony with the customs of one's time. Moreover, like the ancient sceptics, Montaigne found scepticism not only truer but safer. By taking doubt to its limits, by shaking all convictions and holding nothing as certain, Pyrrhonism created the peaceful and free life. Montaigne's counsel was similar to Castellio's in that he argued that the human being must recognize the limitations of reason and accept the life of uncertainty. One should live like the ancient Pyrrhonians who freed themselves from the "passionate sectarianism" by constantly living in "doubt and suspension of judgment."

> Is it not better to remain in doubt than to get entangled in the many errors produced by human fantasy? Is it not better to postpone one's adherence indefinitely than to intervene in factions, both quarreling and seditious . . . is it not better to keep out of the fray altogether?[40]

Repeatedly Montaigne makes clear that we have no criterion for any lasting judgment, no touchstone for distinguishing truth from falsehood. Speaking of the religious conflicts among his fellow Christians he writes, "and meanwhile who will be a proper judge of such differences? It is like saying that we could do with a judge who is not bound to either party in our religious strife, who is dispassionate and without prejudice. Among Christians that cannot be."[41] All of these statements must be read in the context of Montaigne's statements about religion with which he opened the *Apology*. Reflecting the "wars now besetting our country" he argued,

> Think whether we do not take religion into our own hands and twist it like wax into shapes quite opposed to a rule so unbending and direct. Has that ever been so clear as in France today? Some approach it from this side, some from the other, some make it black and others make it white; all are alike in using religion for their violent and ambitious schemes.... Just see the horrifying impudence with which we toss theological arguments to and fro and how irreligiously we cast them off or take them up again. . . . [W]e burn people at the stake for saying truth must bow to our necessities . . .[42]

To promote peace, Montaigne returned to his principle that undermined certainty:

> All this is a clear sign that we accept our religion only as we would fashion it from our own hands—no differently from the way other religions gain acceptance. We happen to be born in a country where it is practiced, or else we have regard for its age and for the authority of the men who have upheld it; perhaps we fear the threats which it attaches to the wicked or go along with its promises. Such considerations as these must be developed in defense of our beliefs as support troops. Their bonds are human. Another religion, other witnesses, similar promises or similar menaces would, in the same way, stamp a contrary belief in us. We are Christians by the same title that we are Perigordians or Germans.[43]

We cannot, Montaigne argued, ever claim any finality. Hence he counseled against the rash certainty of religious knowledge by saying that "there is a plague on man; namely, his opinion that he knows something." Human beings belong to the realm of flux, change, and time and, therefore, "have no communication with being." God alone truly "Is" and "man cannot have thought beyond his reach."[44]

In the end Montaigne and Castellio agreed on the healthy rejection of certitude. Montaigne extended scepticism far beyond Castellio by radically questioning all forms of human knowledge and arguing for the suspension of judgment.[45] However, both men, one Protestant and one Catholic, identified safety and true humanity with the willingness to be limited, to doubt, and to live in peace with uncertainty. Viewing the wreckage of his own time, Montaigne asked, "Why cannot a wise man dare to doubt anything and everything?"[46]

Beyond Montaigne and Castellio stood the towering figure of Shakespeare in whom we find a darker scepticism than that of his predecessors. Montaigne had argued that the mind could not penetrate the divine realm. The mind was unable to reach the essential nature of both God and an ever-changing world. However, in the final book of the *Essays* (1585-1588) he rather cheerfully counseled his readers to turn to a knowledge of the self in order to search for a way to live wisely and well. Seeking a practical morality that befits our proper "rank," Montaigne left his readers with a "self portrait" and a task that he found quite useful.[47]

But Shakespeare's tragedies reflect the Montaigne of the "Apology for Raymond Sebond." Both Montaigne and Shakespeare were intensely determined to strip away human dignity and showing man, including the Renaissance "God-King," who he really was. Both men were relentless in ripping away all the illusions of human nature to reduce man to nothing. As Lear stated, "Nothing will come of nothing."[48]

Like Montaigne (whom he had read), Shakespeare denied that the human mind could find a certain knowledge of God. The inscrutability, hiddenness, and silence of God (or the gods) is most evident in *King Lear*. In his anger and sorrow, Lear cried to the gods, "If you do love old men, if your sweet sway/Allow obedience, if you yourselves are old,/Make it your cause; send down and take my part."[49] Yet even by the end of the play, Lear's answer is expressed only by Gloucester who despairs, "As flies to wanton boys, are we to the gods; they kill us for their sport."[50] By analyzing questions regarding the knowledge and nature of God in *King Lear*, *Hamlet*, *Othello*, and *Troilus and Cressida*, the reader finds that Shakespeare continually portrayed the divine as distant, cold, absent, mute, or irrelevant.

Shakespeare, however, did not then turn to a more contented knowledge of the self. For Shakespeare, knowledge of the self was likewise remote and could be found not by rigorous observation but only by experiencing the most humiliating and harrowing of tragedies. In *King Lear*, *Hamlet*, and *Othello*, self-knowledge is discovered solely through deceit, betrayal, and unimaginable suffering. Only the rejection by his daughters, the experience in the storm, and the death of his beloved Cordelia made Lear recognize himself as the "unaccommodated man." So, too, after Bolinbroke's initial victories, Richard II began to realize that he was nothing more than a man: "Throw away respect,/Tradition, form and ceremonious duty,/ For you have but mistook me all this while./ I live like you, feel want,/taste grief, need friends. Subjected thus,/how can you say to me I am a king?"[51] In the dungeon Richard II finally realized his full humanity. "Think that I am unking'd by Bolinbroke,/ and straight am nothing. But whate'er I be,/ nor I nor any man that man is/With nothing shall be pleas'd, Till he be eas'd/ with being nothing."[52] In a similar vein, the tragic deaths of King Hamlet, Ophelia, and Desdemona brought self-knowledge to Hamlet and Othello.

Nevertheless, Shakespeare's scepticism runs even more deeply. The ultimate human deception lay, for Shakespeare, in the disparity between appearance and reality.[53] Repeatedly Shakespeare presented human life not so much in flux (Montaigne) but as opaque and deceptive, as surface hiding an ugly reality. That which occurs on the surface of life is a cunning illusion that conceals an evil underlying truth. Until those illusory appearances are stripped away through the tragedies of suffering and death, the protagonist cannot penetrate to the true nature of his situation.

The most important illusory appearances which Shakespeare always distrusts are those of power and certitude. *Hamlet* opens with the great disjunction between Claudius's majestic court and the inner reality of corruption and murder. The fact that "something is rotten in the state of Denmark" is hidden under a seemingly healthy exterior. The recurring theme throughout the drama is that a powerful, properly ordered, regal, stately, and outward surface conceals an inward sickness, a "poison," or disease;[54] this imagery is perfect because poison works in a hidden, inward manner. Only Claudius knows the truth. Very gradually Hamlet is driven toward the inner core, toward the reality of the evil that underlies the appearance of order and legitimacy. Polonius's vapid complacency in his own powers of perception function as a parody of Hamlet's continual struggle to find certainty about what is true and what is deceptive: "if circumstances lead me, I will find where truth is hid,/though it were hid indeed/Within the center."[55] In the end Hamlet finds the truth that ultimately causes his death. The close of the play recapitulates this theme of appearance versus reality. Hamlet's final request is one that begs for further revealing of the truth: "O God, Horatio, what a wounded name,/ Things standing thus unknown, shall I leave/behind me!/ If thou didst ever hold me in thy heart,/Absent thee from felicity awhile,/ And in this harsh world draw thy breath in pain,/ To tell my story."[56] And Horatio does take up the dying man's wish and reports the truth "hid indeed within the center." Thus Horatio recounts the occurrence of the situation but in such a way that he portrays the deceptive nature of the many past acts and appearances: "And let me speak to th' yet unknowing world/ How these things came about. So shall you hear/Of carnal, bloody, and unnatural acts,/ Of accidental judgments, casual slaughters,/ of deaths put on by cunning and forc'd cause,/ And, in this upshot, purposes mistook/ Fall'n on th' inventors' heads. All this can I/ Truly deliver."[57]

This painful discovery of the differences between power and impotence, certainty and deception, surface and reality recur in Shakespeare's other major plays. Richard II sees himself as divinely appointed, certain in his legitimate power. The play, however, steadily undercuts the traditional medieval theories surrounding kingship and exposes the frightening political realities that are really at work in the world. Richard and Bolinbroke personify the chasm between appearance and reality. The exposure of this chasm, moreover, is always at the expense of power and certitude. As Richard's power disintegrates, his former certainty of self and position is destroyed. Only as Richard's royal power and identity crumble does he begin to perceive anything of real value. In both *Richard III* and *Othello*, the theme of false certainty is expanded. Both plays portray all human action as manipulated by an unseen, evil, deceptive, secret, scheming power operating behind the scenes and which, in the end, destroys the lives of those whose certainty and power were once intact. In the same way, Edmund and Iago are comparable figures; both engineer disastrous consequences by creating evil, but deceptively true, appearances. In the process of Edmund's machinations, Lear and Gloucester fall from a position of deluded certainty and power to the state of insecure, frightened, poor humanity. Once again, in *King Lear*, power and certitude hide the reality of evil and the real nature of the self. *Othello* follows the same pattern. The formerly powerful and certain warrior is deceived by Iago's secret scheming. Finally, after the death of Desdemona, Othello recognizes the awful truth about the situation and about himself. The falsity of certitude is exemplified by Iago's demonic but true words: "I am not what I am."[58]

In all these works Shakespeare continually linked certainty and power together as surface and illusory appearances because power creates a false and deceptive certitude. When that power disintegrates, the shallowness of its certainty is seen in all of its illusory deceit. At that final and climactic moment when all traditional certainties are stripped away, the true nature of reality appears and one learns the real nature of the self and society. Thus Lear says, "Is man no more than this? Consider him well . . . Thou art the thing itself, unaccommodated man is no more but such a poor, bare, forked animal as thou art." As power crumbles, the superficial order of the surface cracks to reveal the underlying reality of chaos: "If that the heavens do not their visible spirits/ Send quickly down to tame these vile offenses,/ It will come/ Humanity must per force prey upon itself,/ Like monsters of the deep."[59]

As subsequent history testified, Albany's prediction in *King Lear* came true. The divisions and controversies of the time had always been surrounded by violence. On July 1, 1523, the first martyrs of the Reformation were burned to death before the town hall in Brussels. Castellio's attack on certainty was a response to the execution of Servetus. Such executions happened with dismal regularity throughout the sixteenth century, always in the name of one's certain interpretation of Scripture. As David Steinmetz so eloquently stated, "The Bible was on the lips of the religious martyrs—Roman Catholic, Protestant, and Anabaptist—and on the lips of their executioners. In the judgment of sixteenth-century Europeans, the Bible was worth both the dying and the killing for."[60] Moreover, the result of the unsettling political, social, economic, and religious changes that swept through Europe was religious warfare. In August of 1571, the St. Bartholomew's Massacre killed thousands; at the instigation of Catherine dé Medici, between 5,000 and 10,000 Hugenots were killed.[61] When the news of the massacre reached

Spain, Philip II was said to have laughed publicly for the first time in his life. When Trent concluded its decree on certainty, the Thirty Years War was about three decades away. The religious debates also continued to rage on. The intellectual ferment that fueled the controversies of the Reformation era continued into the seventeenth century as Descartes and Pascal tried to formulate answers that attempted to ease the anguished quest for certainty that had come to dominate the intellectual and religious history of the time.

Endnotes

1. Stephen J. Greenblatt, *Renaissance Self-Fashioning from More to Shakespeare* (Chicago: University of Chicago Press, 1980), 88, 113, 219. The citation is from Greenblatt's analysis of *Othello*, 254.

2. *Canons and Decrees of the Council of Trent*, sixth session (1547), Chapter IX and Canon XV: "If anyone says that a man who is reborn and justified is required *ex fide* to believe that he is certainly in the number of the predestined, let him be anathema." Canon XVI reads: "If anyone says that he will for certain, with absolute and infallible certainty, have the great gift of perseverance even to the end, (unless he shall have learned this by a special revelation), let him be anathema." Translation from John H. Leith, ed., *Creeds of the Churches: A Reader in Christian Doctrine from the Bible to the Present*, 3rd edition (Atlanta: John Knox Press, 1982), 413-14, 422. See also: G. des Lauriers, "St Augustin et la question de la certitude de la grâce au Concile de Trente," *Augustinus Magister* I (Paris, 1954), 1051-67; V. Heynck, "Zur Kontroverse über die Gnadengewissheit auf dem Konzil von Trient," *Franziskanische Studien* 37 (1955): 1-17; H. Huthmacher, "La certitude de la grâce au Concile de Trente," *Nouvelle Revue Théologique* 60 (1933): 213-226; Adolf Stakemeier, *Das Konzil von Trient über die Heilsgewissheit* (Heidelberg: F. H. Kerle Verlag, 1947).

3. (WA) Martin Luther, *D. Martin Luthers Werke* (Weinmar: H. Bohlau, 1883-), 43: 459. 25-27; (LW) Martin Luther, *Luther's Works* (Saint Louis: Concordia Publishing House, 1995-), 5: 45.

4. WA 40: 579: 17-22, 589:15-17, 591 :27-28; LW 26: 380, 386, 388.

5. Zwingli, *Refutation of the Tricks of the Catabaptists*, trans. Samuel Macauley Jackson (Philadelphia: University of Pennsylvania Press, 1901), 242. Latin edition is found in Z III. 357-437. See also: Zwingli, *De providentia Dei*, Z VI/iii. 178, 9-10. See Also *De providentia Dei* Z VI/iii.22-184.17; Z VI/i. 178.6-7. English translation can be found in, Zwingli, *Zwingli. On Providence and Other Essays*, (Durham: The Labyrinth Press 1983), 197-200.

6. *Institutes*, III. 2.7. All citations are from *Institutes of the Christian Religion*, John T. McNeil, ed. and trans. Ford Lewis Battles, Vols. XX-XXI, The Library of Christian Classics (Philadelphia: Westminster Press, 1975).

7. *Institutes*, III. 2.15.

8. *De providentia Dei*, Z VI/iii.180.8-27; *On Providence*, 199.

9. *Institutes,* III. 1.3, 2.11-12, 15-16, 34, 37, 39.

10. *Institutes*, III. 1.3-4; Also: m. 2.11; m.2. 15-16.

11. For some examples of studies on exegesis in the Reformation era, see: David C. Steinmetz, *Luther in Context* (Bloomington: Indiana University Press, 1986); *idem*, "Theology and Exegesis: Ten Theses" and "Discussion Agenda for the Session on

Theology and Exegesis" in *Histoire de l'exégèse au XVIe siècle. Etudes de philologie et d'histoire* 34 (Geneva: Librairie Droz, 1978), 383-384; *idem* "Hermeneutic and Old Testament Interpretation in Staupitz and the Young Martin Luther," *Archiv für Reformationsgeschichte* 70 (1979): 24-58; *idem*, "John Calvin on Isaiah 6: A Problem in the History of Exegesis," *Interpretation* 36 (April, 1982): 156-170; idem, *The Bible in the Sixteenth Century* (Durham and London: Duke University Press, 1990); *idem*, *Calvin in Context* (New York and Oxford: Oxford University Press, 1995); Scott H. Hendrix, *Tradition and Authority in the Reformation* (Aldershot Hampshire, Great Britain: Variorum, 1996), 229-239; Richard A. Muller and John L. Thompson, *Biblical Interpretation in the Era of the Reformation: Essays Presented to David C. Steinmetz in Honor of His Sixtieth Birthday* (Grand Rapids and Cambridge, U. K.: William B. Eerdmans Publishing Company, 1996); Richard A. Muller, *The Unaccommodated Calvin: Studies in the Foundation of a Theological Tradition* (New York and Oxford: Oxford University Press, 2000); Timothy J. Wengert, *Philip Melanchthon's 'Annotationes in Johannem' in Relation to Its Predecessors and Contemporaries,* Travaux d'Humanisme et Renaissance CCXX (Geneva: Librairie Droz, 1987); Susan E. Schreiner, *Where Shall Wisdom Be Found? Calvin's Exegesis of Job from Medieval and Modern Perspectives* (Chicago and London: University of Chicago Press, 1994).

12. The phrase "exegetical optimism" is from David C. Steinmetz, *Luther in Context*, 96. See also Steinmetz's essay, "Scripture and the Lord's Supper in Luther's Theology," in idem., *Luther in Context*, 72-84; Brian A. Gerrish, "Gospel and Eucharist: John Calvin on the Lord's Supper," and "Sign and Reality: The Lord's Supper in the Reformed Confessions," in *The Old Protestantism and the New: Essays on the Reformation Heritage* (Edinburgh: T. & T. Clark, 1982), 106-130. On the important topic of authority in general see, Gillian R. Evans, *Problems of Authority in the Reformation Debates* (Cambridge: Cambridge University Press, 1992).

13. Heiko A. Oberman, *The Dawn of the Reformation: Essays in Late Medieval and Early Reformation Thought* (Edinburgh: T. & T. Clark, 1986), 285. Scott Hendrix argues that the Reformers accepted a limited authority of the Fathers, an authority always below the authority of Scripture. According to Hendrix, the Reformers felt a "theological freedom" to appropriate or to criticize the writings of the ancient Fathers. As Luther insisted at the Marburg Colloquy, Scripture's authority demanded that he say the fathers erred before he would abandon God's Word. See Scott H. Hendrix, *Tradition and Authority in the Reformation*, 55-68. On defenses of Luther's "objectivity" see, Michael Baylor, *Action and Person: Conscience in Late Scholasticism and the Young Luther* (Leiden: E. J. Brill, 1977), 267; Regin Prenter, *Spiritus Creator*, trans. John Jensen (Philadelphia: Muhlenberg Press, 1946), 247-308; Brian A. Gerrish, *Continuing the Reformation: Essays on Modern Religious Thought* (Chicago: University of Chicago Press, 1993), 38-56.

14. George Huntston Williams, *The Radical Reformation*, 3rd ed. (Kirksville: Sixteenth Century Essays and Studies, 1992), 1248-1249.

15. Susan E. Schreiner, "The Spiritual Man Judges All Things, Calvin and Exegetical Debates about Certainty in the Reformation," in *Biblical Interpretation in the Era of the Reformation*, 189-215.

16. For an analysis of these thinkers see, Steven E. Ozment, *Mysticism and Dissent: Religious Ideology and Social Protest in the Sixteenth Century* (New Haven: Yale University Press, 1973).

17. Thomas Müntzer, *The Collected Works of Thomas Müntzer*, trans. and ed. by Peter Matheson (Edinburgh: T. & T. Clark), 223-24, see also 198-99.

18. Cited by Ozment, *Mysticism and Dissent*, 122.

19. Ozment, *Mysticism and Dissent*, 121-122. For a discussion of Anabaptist hermeneutical principles see Williams, *The Radical Reformation*, 1255-1260.

20. Cited by Williams, *The Radical Reformation*, 1249.

21. Cited by Ozment, *Mysticism and Dissent*, 149-150.

22. These are statements made by Luther who is repeating the accusations of his opponents: WA 45: 728. 19-24; LW 24: 293.

23. Johann Eck, *Enchiridion locorum communium adversus Lutherum et alios hostes ecclesiae*, I. 4; ed. P. Fraenkel, *Corpus Catholicorum* 34. English edition can be found in: Johann Eck, *Enchiridion of Commonplaces: Against Luther and Other Enemies of the Church*, trans. Ford Lewis Battles (Grand Rapids: Baker Book House, 1979).

24. Thomas More, *Responsio ad Lutherum* in *The Complete Works of St. Thomas More*, vol. 5, ed. John Headley, trans. by Sister Scholastica Mandeville (New Haven: Yale University Press, 1969), 185.

25. Eck, *Enchiridion*, I.1.

26. Thomas More, *The Confutation of Tyndale's Answer*, in *The Complete Works of Thomas More*, Vol. 8/II, 575.

27. Eck, *Enchiridion*, Widmungsvorrede, 8 and chapter I.

28. Eck, *Enchiridion*, IV.3.

29. "Creed of the Council of Trent," in *Creeds of the Churches*, 440.

30. Susan E. Schreiner, *Unmasking the Angel of Light: The Problem of Deception in Martin Luther and Teresa of Avila*, forthcoming from the University of Chicago Press.

31. The standard work on Castellio is Ferdinand E. Buisson, *Sébastien Castellion. sa vie et son oeuvre (1515-1563)* 2 vols. (Paris: Hachette, 1892).

32. For discussions on tolerance during this era see Joseph Lecler, S.J., *Toleration and the Reformation*, 2 vols. (London: Longmans, 1960); Roland H. Bainton, "The Development and Consistency of Luther's Attitude to Religious Liberty," *Harvard Theological Review* XXII (1929): 107-149; *idem*, "The Parable of the Tares as the Proof Text for Religious Liberty to the End of the Sixteenth Century," *Church History* I (1932): 67-89; *idem*, *Travail of Religious Liberty* (New York: Harper, 1958); Ch. Bost, "Sébastien Castellion et l'opposition protestante contre Calvin," *Revue de Théologie et de Philosophie* (1914): 301-321; Nikolaus Paulus, *Protestantismus und Toleranz im 16. Jahrhundert von Nikolaus Paulus* (Freiberg im Breisgau: 1911); Johannes Kühn, "Das Geschichtsproblem der Toleranz," *Autour de Michel Servet et de Sébastien Castellion* ed. Bruno Becker (Haarlem: H.D. Tjeenk Willink, 1953), 1-28. For a more recent approach see, *Tolerance and Intolerance in the European Reformation*, ed. Ole Peter Grell and Bob Scribner (Cambridge: Cambridge University Press, 1996).

33. Sebastian Castellio, *Concerning Heretics*, trans. Roland Bainton (New York: Columbia University Press, 1935), 297-298.

34. Ibid., 215.

35. In 1563, Castellio wrote a treatise on this subject, *De arte dubitandi et confidendi ignorandi et sciendi* now in a critical edition with introduction and notes by Elisabeth Feist Hirsch (Leiden: E. J. Brill, 1981).

36. Castellio, *Concerning Heretics*, 241.

37. Castellio, "Reply to Calvin" in *Concerning Heretics*, 281-282.

38. Castellio, "Concerning Doubt and Belief, Ignorance and Knowledge" in *Concerning Heretics*, 288. Castellio continues (289) to say, "There are some who are unwilling to doubt anything, to be in ignorance of anything. They assert everything, unreservedly, and if you dissent from them they damn you without hesitation. . . . Solomon says in Ecclesiastes, 'To everything there is a season, and a time and purpose under heaven; a time to be born and a time to die; a time to plant, and a time to

pluck up what has been planted,' . . . In the same way, I say there is a time to doubt and a time to believe; a time to be ignorant and a time to know . . . To hold the uncertain for certain and to entertain no doubt on the point is rash and dangerous."

39. Citations are from Michel de Montaigne, *An Apology for Raymond Sebond*, trans. and ed. M. A. Screech (London: Penguin Press, 1987).

40. Ibid., 71.

41. Ibid., 185.

42. Ibid., 6-8.

43. Ibid., 8.

44. Ibid., 91, 188-189.

45. Ibid., 70.

46. Ibid., 71.

47. Donald M. Frame, *Montaigne: A Biography* (New York: Harcourt, Brace & World, Inc., 1965), 246-323.

48. W. B. Drayton Henderson, "Montaigne's Apologie of Raymond Sebond and King Lear," *The Shakespeare Association Bulletin* 14, no. 4 (Oct., 1939): 209-225.

49. *King Lear* II. IV. 189-191. All citations are from *The Complete Works of Shakespeare*, 3rd edition, ed. David Bevington (Glenview, IL and London: Scott, Foresman and Company 1980).

50. *King Lear,* IV. I. 36-37.

51. *Richard II,* III. II. 172-177.

52. *Richard II*, V. VI. 37-41.

53. The best treatment of this subject remains that by Theodore Spencer, *Shakespeare and the Nature of Man* (New York: The Macmillan Company, 1942).

54. Caroline Spurgeon, *Shakespeare's Imagery and What It Tells Us* (Cambridge: Cambridge University Press, 1935).

55. *Hamlet*, II. II. 156-158. Also see Bevington's remarks in the introduction on page 1070.

56. *Hamlet*, V. II. 346-352.

57. *Hamlet*, I. II. 381-388.

58. *Othello*, I. I. 66. See also, Greenblatt, *Renaissance Self-Fashioning*, 236.

59. *King Lear*, IV. II. 47-51.

60. David C. Steinmetz, *Luther in Context*, 45.

61. Barbara B. Diefendorf, *Beneath the Cross: Catholics and Huguenots in Sixteenth Century Paris* (New York and Oxford: Oxford University Press, 1991).

Could God Not Sorrow If We Do?
Nicholas Wolterstorff

YALE UNIVERSITY DIVINITY SCHOOL
NEW HAVEN, CONNECTICUT

Scripture's Representation of God—and the Philosophers' Response

God is represented in Hebrew and Christian Scripture as one who has a history of action, knowledge, disturbance, and response. Recall Exodus 3 and 4. When Moses was tending the herds of his father-in-law in the wilderness, his curiosity was piqued one day by a bush engulfed in flames but not consumed. He walked over, and as he approached, God addressed him out of the bush, "Moses, Moses" (Ex 3:4). It is the narrator who tells us that it was God addressing him; Moses does not yet know what to make of what is happening. Moses responded, "Here I am" (Ex 3:4). Whereupon God said, "Come no closer! Remove the sandals from your feet, for the place on which you are standing is holy ground" (Ex 3:5). The speaker in the bush then identified himself: "I am the God of your father, the God of Abraham, the God of Isaac, and the God of Jacob" (Ex 3:6). Moses was gripped by fear, and no longer daring to look, covered his face.

God then tells Moses that he has seen the affliction of his people, has heard their cry, knows their sufferings, and has come down to deliver them from servitude and bring them into a land where they can flourish. So come, says God, "I will send you to Pharaoh to bring my people, the Israelites, out of Egypt" (Ex 3:10).

What then follows is a series of protests by Moses. Who am I that I should go to Pharaoh and lead my people out? I will be with you, says God. But if I tell my people that the God of their fathers has sent me to lead them out, they will want to know your name. Tell them that *I AM WHO I AM*, says God. But they will not believe me when I tell them that you appeared and spoke to me. As a sign, I will enable you to perform some wonders, says God. But I am a poor speaker. I will give you the right words to speak when they are needed, says God. But I just do not want to do it; pick someone else.

No, says God, angry now; I will appoint your brother Aaron to speak for you in public; but you are to be the leader.

This incident stands out as one of the great numinous episodes in the biblical literature. But in its representation of God as one who has a history of action, knowledge, disturbance, and response, it is not exceptional but typical. The God of Scripture is one of whom a narrative can be told; we know that not because Scripture says so, but because Scripture offers such a narrative.

While of course recognizing that this is how Scripture represents God, the philosophers and theologians of the mainline Christian tradition, and of a significant strand in the Jewish tradition, have nonetheless held that this is not how God in fact is. God does indeed act and know; but God is neither disturbed, nor does God respond; and God has no history.

Let me now articulate a methodological principle for the development of Christian theology which I accept and which, so it appears to me, the bulk of Christian theologians also tacitly, if not explicitly, accept: an implication of accepting Scripture as canonical is that one affirm, as literally true, Scripture's representation of God unless, on some point, one has good reason not to do so.[1] Put it like this: the burden of proof, for those who accept Scripture as canonical, is on those who hold that Scripture's representation of God is not literally true at some point.

All Christians and Jews believe, concerning some aspects of Scripture's representation of God, that there are good reasons for not affirming those aspects as literally true. All believe that on some points the burden of proof can be borne. For example, Scripture on occasion represents God as having wings; nobody affirms that representation as literally true. It will be agreed that the representation *points* to something true, but God is not among the literally winged things of reality.

It is appropriate to ask whether the massiveness of the Christian theological tradition against taking as literally true Scripture's representation of God as having a history of action, knowledge, disturbance, and response, has not shifted the burden of proof so that, for present-day Christian philosophers and theologians, it lies on those who hold that the representation, in this regard, is literally true. No, it has not; it has not shifted the burden of proof. What it has done, in my judgment, is place on those who disagree with the theological tradition a weighty obligation. We are obligated to understand as deeply and sympathetically as we can the considerations offered by our predecessors in favor of not taking the representation as literally true. The burden of proof remains on them, however. Accepting Scripture as canonical implies at least this.

In this essay I wish to consider whether there are good reasons for Christian philosophers and theologians not to take as literally true Scripture's representation of God as often disturbed by what transpires in human affairs, good reasons for regarding God, contrary to the biblical representation, as invulnerably and imperturbably happy. I propose following my own advice concerning procedure. Rather than treating the matter ahistorically, I shall consider what Thomas Aquinas, one of the giants of the Christian philosophical and theological tradition, had to say on the matter. For present-day Jewish philosophers and theologians a closely parallel discussion could be conducted by considering what Maimonides had to say.

One finds it said in many quarters nowadays that God suffers. Often the persons who say this, though Christian, seem unaware of the near-unanimity of the Christian tradition in favor of the opposite view; even when not unaware, all too often they offer reasons against the traditional view that the philosophers and theologians of the tradition would find ludicrously simplistic. For example: since God loves human beings, since empathy is an important part of love, since there is suffering among human beings, and since empathy with the suffering is itself a mode of suffering, God must suffer. I too am of the view that God is disturbed by what happens within creation. But I shall do what I can to earn my right to disagree with the tradition. Of course a full treatment of the matter would have to go beyond Aquinas to consider whether perhaps other philosophers and theologians succeeded in bearing the burden. All we can do on this occasion is scrutinize Aquinas's argumentation.

The Issue for Aquinas: not Passion but Sorrow

Let us begin by locating the issue. In the course of his discussion of God's love in Question 20 of Part I of his *Summa theologica*,

Aquinas distinguishes between love, joy, and delight as *passions*,
and love, joy, and delight as *acts of the intellective appetite*. He then
says that love, joy, and delight, though not present in God as passions, are present in God as aspects of God's intellective appetite
(1.*ad* 1). He goes on to say:

> As regards the formal element of certain passions,
> a certain imperfection is implied, as in desire, which
> is of the good we have not, and in sorrow (*tristitia*),
> which is about the evil we have. This applies also to
> anger, which supposes sorrow. Certain other
> passions, however, as love and joy, imply no
> imperfection. Since therefore none of these can be
> attributed to God on their material side, . . . neither
> can those that even on their formal side imply
> imperfection be attributed to Him; except
> metaphorically, and from likeness of effects. . . .
> Whereas those that do not imply imperfection, such
> as love and joy, can be properly predicated of God,
> though without attributing passion to Him . . . (1.*ad*
> 2).[2]

For those of us who read this passage without prior acquaintance with Aquinas's philosophical psychology, there is much that
is obscure and in need of explanation; shortly I will be giving the
explanation. But let me state the main point: Aquinas holds that
the same distinction can be made for desire, sorrow, and anger that
he invited us to make for love, joy and delight; namely, we can distinguish between desire, sorrow, and anger understood as *passions*,
and desire, sorrow, and anger understood as *acts of the intellective
appetite*. And his thesis is that whereas love, joy, and delight *qua*
aspects of the intellective appetite can be "properly predicated" of
God, though not *qua passions*, desire, sorrow, and anger cannot be
predicated of God even *qua* aspects of the intellective appetite; they
can only be predicated of God "metaphorically," for the reason that
whereas love, joy, and delight taken thus "do not imply imperfection," desire, sorrow, and anger inherently "imply imperfection."

Before we explore Aquinas's philosophical psychology so as to
understand better how he is thinking here, let us have before us a
passage from his *Summa contra gentiles* in which he makes the
same point concerning the presence of joy in God and the absence of
sorrow, but does so with a slightly different conceptual apparatus:

Some passions . . . are excluded from God not only by reason of their genus, but also by reason of their species. For every passion is specified by its object. That passion, therefore, whose subject is absolutely unfitting to God is removed from God even according to the nature of its proper species. Such a passion...is *sorrow* or *pain* (*tristitia* or *dolor*), for its subject is the already present evil, just as the object of *joy* is the good present and possessed. Sorrow and pain, therefore, of their very nature cannot be found in God (I.89.8-9).

There are certain passions which, though they do not befit God as passions, do not signify anything by the nature of their species that is repugnant to the divine perfection. Among these passions are *joy* and *delight* (*gaudium* and *delectatio*). Delight is of a present good. Neither, therefore, by reason of its object, which is a good, nor by reason of its disposition towards its object, which is possessed in act, is joy, according to the nature of its species, repugnant to the divine perfection. From this it is manifest that joy or delight is properly in God (I.90.1-3).

The place to begin articulating the relevant part of Aquinas's philosophical psychology is with his concept of appetite, and then with his distinction between two kinds of appetite: sensitive and intellective. Appetite is the faculty for attaching oneself to something, loving it, investing oneself in it. It is important that it not be identified with desire. Whereas desire is appetite for some "good we have not," not all appetite is for goods we have not; one may *possess* some good for which one has appetite. If so, one experiences joy or delight, the object of the joy being "the good present and possessed."[3]

When the object of an act of appetite is apprehended by sense, then the appetite is *sensitive* appetite; when it is apprehended (solely) by the intellect, then the appetite is *intellective* appetite (*S.th.* I.80.2.*resp*). An example of an act of sensitive appetite would be a person's desire for some food that she sees; examples of acts of intellective appetite would be one's desire for such things as knowledge, virtue, and God (*S.th.* I.80.2.*ad* 2).[4]

Having drawn this distinction, Aquinas then makes the crucial move of identifying sensitive appetites with passions (see especially

S.th. I-II.22.2). Passions, he says, "are movements of the sensitive appetite" (*S.th.* I-II.23.1.*sed contra*). It follows, of course, that only embodied agents can have passions; one needs a body if one is to have a sensory apparatus. But the involvement of the body in the passions is much more intimate, in Aquinas's view, than just that one's apprehension of the thing desired is by way of the senses. The "movement" involved in a passion always involves some sort of bodily change; "for example, the contraction or distension of the heart, or something of the sort" (*S.c.g.* I.89.3). It may, in fact, have been Aquinas's view that such bodily disturbance belongs to the *nature* of the passions; that is the natural way to interpret his comment that "acts of the sensitive appetite, inasmuch as they have annexed to them some bodily change, are called passions" (*S.th.* I.20.1.*ad* 1).[5]

Given Aquinas's way of structuring the terrain, the question of whether God has passions is of no interest. Since passions are sensitive appetites, and God has no body, God obviously has no passions; "in God and the angels there is no sensitive appetite" (*S.th.* I-II.24.3.*ad* 2).

Of equal importance with Aquinas's identification of acts of the sensitive appetites with passions is his identification of the intellective (or intellectual) appetite with the will (see especially *S.th.* I.82). The "intellectual appetite . . . is called the will," he says (*S.th.* I.82.2.*obj* 3).

Aquinas does not identify will as such with *free will*, however. Will as such is that faculty whereby we love, attach ourselves to, invest ourselves in, something that we judge to be good. *Free will* is a special type of will—that is, a special type of intellective appetite. The *power* of free will "is nothing else but the power of choice" (*S.th.* I.83.4.*resp*); and "to choose is to desire something for the sake of obtaining something else" (*ibid*). Accordingly, an *act* of free will is the desiring of something one has chosen—that is to say, the desiring of something for the sake of obtaining something else. An act of free will presupposes a judgment concerning means to desired ends.

Aquinas is not of the view that choice occurs when desire reaches a certain point of intensity, perhaps 8.5 on the rheostat of desire. Nor is he of the view that choice consists in selecting which, among one's desires, will function as motive for action. Choice, to say it again, is desiring something as means to some other desire one has; and free will is the *capacity* for thus choosing. Aquinas explains his thought nicely in the *respondeo* of *Summa theologica* I.83.3:

> the proper act of free will is choice; for we say that we have a free will because we can take one thing while refusing another; and this is to choose. Therefore we must consider the nature of free will, by considering the nature of choice. Now two things concur in choice: one on the part of the cognitive power, the other on the part of the appetitive power. On the part of the cognitive power, counsel is required, by which we judge one thing to be preferred to another; and on the part of the appetitive power, it is required that the appetite should accept the judgment of counsel.

We have already seen that God and the angels have intellective appetite. Aquinas is explicit in affirming that they thus have will:

> Love, concupiscence, and the like can be understood in two ways. Sometimes they are taken as passions—arising, that is, with a certain commotion of the soul. . . . [I]n this sense they are only in the sensitive appetite. They may, however, be taken in another way, as far as they are simple affections without passion or commotion of the soul, and thus they are acts of the will. And in this sense, too, they are attributed to the angels and to God (*S.th.* I.82.5.*ad* 1).

It is now clear how Aquinas was thinking when he said that joy or delight "is properly in God," and that love and joy "can be properly predicated of God." In the first place, though God has no passion, God does have intellective appetite: "when love and joy and the like are ascribed to God or the angels, or to man in respect of his intellectual appetite, they signify simple acts of the will having like effects, but without passion" (*S.th.* I-II.22.3.*ad* 3). Secondly, joy occurs when the object of appetite is "a good present and possessed," whereas sorrow, by contrast, occurs when the object of appetite is an "already present evil" (*S.c.g.* I.89.9). And thirdly, at least some of the good which is an object of God's intellective appetite is "present and possessed." It follows that God experiences the joy which ensues upon satisfied intellective appetite.[6]

Why, for Aquinas, No Sorrow in God?

We are now ready for the main question: Why does Aquinas hold that there is no sadness, no sorrow, in God—no negativity in God's intellective appetite? What are his reasons for departing, in this regard, from the biblical representation of God?

As I read the history of Christian theology, it was especially two convictions that drove the theologians and philosophers of the tradition to the conviction that God has no history of action, knowledge, disturbance, and response. (The same was true of the medieval Jewish tradition as represented by Maimonides.) One was the conviction that God is the ultimate condition of everything not identical with God, and is in no way himself conditioned. The other was the conviction that God is the sole intrinsic good and is in no way himself deficient in excellence. Though the first of these definitely played some role in the traditional argumentation for the conviction that God experiences no disturbance, the dominant role was played by the second. Aquinas was typical in this regard. Let me on this occasion limit myself to the role played in Aquinas's thought by the thesis that God is the sole intrinsic good and in no way himself deficient in excellence.

I must explain what I mean by "intrinsic good." Though in contemporary ethics the concept of the *intrinsically good* is regularly identified with the concept of *that which is an end in itself*, for our purposes here it will be important to distinguish them. The concept of an *end in itself* pertains to the structure of desire: something is an end in itself for a given person at a given time if it is at that time desired by that person for its own sake and not merely as a means to something else. The concept of the *intrinsically good* pertains, by contrast, to the structure of excellence: something good is *intrinsically* good if its excellence is not grounded in some relation it bears to something else which is good. If its excellence is so grounded, then it is *extrinsically* good.

In his thought about the structure of excellence, Aquinas was working with the adaptation of the Platonic picture already worked out by Augustine. The paradigmatically good being is not that impersonal Platonic form, The Good Itself, but is rather God. God's excellence is intrinsic; the excellence of everything else is extrinsic, consisting in some particular relation of similarity that the entity bears to God. What we want to see is how Aquinas uses this framework to argue for the conclusion that God experiences no sadness.

As with joy, so also with sorrow, we must be sure to distinguish the sorrow arising from the sensitive appetite, which is a passion, from the sorrow arising from the intellective appetite (*S.th.* I-II.35.1.*resp*). Just by virtue of knowing that God has no body, we know that the former sort is not a feature of God's experience. But neither can the latter be. Sorrow by its "very nature cannot be found in God" (*S.c.g.* I.89.9), says Aquinas.

Why is that? Well, sorrow implies an "imperfection," and it is for that reason that it cannot "be properly predicated of God" (*S.th.* I.20.1.*ad* 2). Sorrow "is caused by a present evil; and this evil, from the very fact that it is repugnant to the movement of the will, depresses the soul, inasmuch as it hinders it from enjoying that which it wishes to enjoy" (*S.th.* I-II.37.2.*resp*). The "mere fact of a man's appetite being uneasy about a present evil, is [thus] itself an evil, because it hinders the repose of the appetite in good" (*S.th.* I-II.39.1.*resp*). Considered "simply and in itself . . . all sorrow is an evil" (*ibid*). And evil is, of course, "the opposite of good. But the nature of the good consists in perfection, which means that the nature of evil consists in imperfection. Now, in God, who is universally perfect . . . , there cannot be defect or imperfection. Therefore evil cannot be in God." "Evil, which is the opposite of good, could have no place in God" (*S.c.g.* I.39.5 and 3). Hence sorrow could have no place in God.[7]

Aquinas sometimes presents this line of thought as if he regarded it as a good argument, all by itself, for the conclusion that in God there is no sorrow or sadness. In one passage, however, he points out why it is not that. Though sorrow as such is a deficiency in excellence, that is to say, an evil, to determine whether someone's sorrowing over something represents a deficiency in the excellence *of that person* one has to consider whether perhaps the person is sorrowing over something which calls to be sorrowed over. If so, then the sorrowing represents an *excellence* in that person, not a deficiency; *failure* to sorrow over that would be an evil. Here is how Aquinas makes the point: a thing may be good or evil not just "considered simply and in itself," but "on the supposition of something else: thus shame is said to be good, on the supposition of a shameful deed done. . . . Accordingly, supposing the presence of something

saddening or painful, it is a sign of goodness if a man is in sorrow or
pain on account of this present evil. For if he were not to be in sorrow or pain, this could only be either because he feels it not, or
because he does not reckon it as something unbecoming, both of
which are manifest evils. Consequently it is a condition of goodness, that, supposing an evil to be present, sorrow or pain should
ensue" (*S.th.* I-II.39.1.*resp*). "Sorrow is a good inasmuch as it denotes perception and rejection of evil" (*S.th.* I-II.39.2.*resp*).

The point is of sufficient importance to bear repeating: a person's
sadness may be an *excellence* in that person, not a *deficiency* in
excellence, not an evil.

It follows from the above that for Aquinas to hold that there is
no sorrow in God, he must hold that there's nothing for God to sorrow over. He must hold that for God, there is no "present evil." And
this is what he does hold—explicitly so.

It is what he had in mind when he said, in the second of the two
passages from which we set out, that sorrow is "absolutely unfitting to God" on account of "the nature of its proper species." The
passage began with Aquinas's remark that all passions are excluded
from God by reason of their genus. We know now what that means.
Passions belong to the genus: *acts of the sensitive appetite.* Since
God has no sensitive appetite, God can have no passions. Some passions are in addition excluded from God on account of their species.
The species of a passion is determined by its object; "every passion
is specified by its object."[8] The passions of joy and delight are "repugnant to the divine perfection" only on account of their genus,
not on account of their species, which is to say, not on account of
their object; hence it is that joy and delight arising from the intellective appetite can be, and are, present in God.[9] But the passions
of sorrow and sadness are "repugnant to the divine perfection" not
only on account of their genus but also on account of their species,
which is determined by their object.

The same point was made, with different conceptuality, in the
first of the two passages from which we set out. Distinguish the
"material side" of the passions from the "formal element." The material side consists in their being acts of the sensitive appetite; the
formal element is determined by the object of the passion. None of
the passions "can be attributed to God on their material side." When

it comes to the formal side, however, we must distinguish. Some imply "a certain imperfection" in their formal element, some do not. Desire and sorrow are of the former sort, desire being "of the good we have not," sorrow being "about the evil we have." Love and joy are of the latter sort; they "imply no imperfection." Accordingly, not only the material side of desire and sorrow, but also the formal side, gives us ground for denying that they can be "properly predicated" of God; the imperfection which they "imply" is incompatible with the divine perfection. By contrast, love and joy can be properly predicated of God, just provided that we don't understand ourselves, in so doing, as "attributing passion" to God but only intellective appetite.

If There Are Evils in the World, then Why No Sorrow in God?

Isn't it just preposterous for Aquinas to hold that there is nothing for God to sorrow over, given all the evils in the world? One possibility to consider is that God is unaware of evils. Aquinas remarks that "just as two things are requisite for pleasure; namely, conjunction with good and perception of this conjunction; so also two things are requisite for pain; namely, conjunction with some evil (which is in so far evil as it deprives one of some good), and perception of this conjunction" (*S.th*. I-II.35.1.*resp*).

Aquinas does not dismiss out of hand the suggestion that God has no knowledge of evils. He takes it seriously enough to discuss it with care in the course of his treatment of God's knowledge, both in the *Summa theologica* and in the *Summa contra gentiles* (*S.th*. I.14.10; *S.c.g*. I.71). His answer is the same in both cases: God does know evils.

The options available to Aquinas for escaping the trap of contradiction are now becoming few indeed. Sorrow is absent from God because there is nothing over which it is appropriate for God to sorrow. Yet beyond a doubt there are evils in the world, and God knows them. Pretty clearly the only way out is for Aquinas to hold that there is no evil for which there is the (unsatisfied) desire in God that that evil be removed or not have appeared. The evils of the world do not constitute a frustration of God's intellective appetite.

Hence it is that God's knowlege of them produces no sorrow or sadness on God's part.

How can Aquinas, with any plausibility, hold such a view? Well, let us begin by reminding ourselves of how Aquinas, along with almost the entire classical and medieval tradition of the West, understood evil. In a human being, inability to see is an evil; it is not that, however, in, say, a sunflower. Similarly, inability to fly is an evil in a mature robin, but not in an ostrich.

Only when we know a thing's proper formation or functioning can we know what for it, or in it, is an evil. An evil in a thing, or for a thing, is a lack, an absence, in the proper formation or functioning of that thing. A properly formed and functioning human being is able to see; that is why inability to see—blindness—is an evil in a human being, whereas of course it is nothing of the sort in a sunflower. A properly formed and functioning mature robin is able to fly; that is why inability to fly is an evil in a robin, whereas, given the stubby wings of properly formed ostriches, it is obviously not an evil in ostriches.

What must be added is that the proper functioning of one thing may be impaired by the proper functioning of another. The snake is undoubtedly functioning properly when it seizes and swallows the fledgling robin; nonetheless, being swallowed by a snake impairs, to put it mildly, the proper functioning of the robin.

With this understanding of evil in hand, let us now turn to some of the things Aquinas says about the divine will. And let us recall that he *identifies* will with the intellective appetite. Will is love for, investment in, and attachment to, something one judges to be good.

In Part I-II, question 39, article 2, of the *Summa theologica*, Aquinas remarks that "Some things do actually happen, not because God wills, but because He permits them to happen—such as sins" (*ad* 3). The same point had been made much earlier, in Part I of the *Summa*, question 19, article 9, where Aquinas asked whether God wills evils. His answer was that God does not will evils but permits them. Speaking again of moral evil, he says that "God . . . neither wills evil to be done, nor wills it not to be done, but wills to permit evil to be done; and this is a good" (*ad* 3).

That last point, about the *good* of God's permission of moral evil, had been developed in the main body of the article:

> Since evil is opposed to good, it is impossible that
> any evil, as such, should be sought for by the
> appetite, either natural, or animal, or by the
> intellectual appetite which is the will. Nevertheless
> evil may be sought accidentally, so far as it
> accompanies a good, as appears in each of the
> appetites. For a natural agent intends not privation
> or corruption, but the form to which is annexed the
> privation of some other form, and the generation of
> one thing, which implies the corruption of another.
> Also when a lion kills a stag, his object is food, to
> obtain which the killing of the animal is only the
> means. Similarly, the fornicator has merely pleasure
> for his object, and the deformity of sin is only an
> accompaniment. . . . Now God wills no good more
> than He wills his own goodness; yet he wills one
> good more than another. Hence He in no way wills
> the evil of sin, which is the privation of right order
> towards the divine good. The evil of natural defect,
> or of punishment, He does will, by willing the good
> to which such evils are attached.

Let me paraphrase the main thought, beginning with Aquinas's thoughts concerning natural evil. God wills certain natural goods more than others—the good of the snake at a certain time, let us say, more than the good of the robin. An inevitable consequence of this is that God often wills some natural evil to a thing—wills, for example, the evil of the impairment of the robin's ability to fly off. Always in such cases the evil that God wills is the consequence, or accompaniment, of some good that God wills. God does not will any natural evil—any impairment of proper formation or functioning—for its own sake.

In the moral domain there are also certain evils that God wills, punishment for sin, for example. The unpleasantness and pain which the punishing act imposes on a person is definitely an evil, that is, an impairment of proper formation or functioning. God wills that evil. Not for its own sake, however, but for the sake of the good to which this evil "is attached." By contrast, God does not in any way will moral evil, that is, the sins that human beings perform. God permits such evils, for the sake of some good achieved by such permission, the goodness of free will being, presumably, primary among such goods.

The question inescapably arises: Granted that God permits sin rather than willing it, is sin nonetheless out of accord with God's will or isn't it? Aquinas's answer is that it *is* out of accord with God's will: "all evil of sin, though happening in many ways, agrees in being out of harmony with the divine will" (*S.th*. I.19.12.*ad* 4).

In saying this, Aquinas would seem to have gotten himself into a double pinch. For let us recall that in our case and God's alike, Aquinas identifies will—not *free* will but *will* as such—with intellective appetite. Accordingly, if something is out of accord with God's will, then perforce it is out of accord with God's intellective appetite. But given the earlier account of sorrow, holding that things happen that are out of harmony with the divine will straightforwardly implies, does it not, that there is sorrow in God? Secondly, given God's omnipotence, how could anything possibly be out of harmony with God's will?

Aquinas attempts to escape the pinch by drawing a distinction between God's *antecedent* will and God's *consequent* will. When he said that sin is out of accord with the divine will, what he meant was that it is out of accord with God's *antecedent* will, not that it is out of accord with God's *consequent* will.

The topic of *Summa theologica* I.19.6 is whether the will of God is always fulfilled. The answer Aquinas develops is that it is, provided it is God's *consequent* will that one has in mind. If one is thinking instead of God's *antecedent* will, then what has to be said is that what God "wills antecedently may not take place" (*ad* 1). The distinction is best explained by quoting Aquinas's own words:

> [E]verything, in so far as it is good, is willed by God.
> A thing taken in its primary sense, and absolutely
> considered, may be good or evil, and yet when some
> additional circumstances are taken into account, by
> a consequent consideration may be changed into the
> contrary. Thus that a man should live is good; and
> that a man should be killed is evil, absolutely
> considered. But if in a particular case we add that a
> man is a murderer or dangerous to society, to kill
> him is a good; that he live is an evil. Hence it may
> be said of a just judge, that antecedently he wills all
> men to live; but consequently wills the murderer to
> be hanged. In the same way God antecedently wills
> all men to be saved, but consequently wills some to

be damned, as His justice exacts. Nor do we will simply, what we will antecedently, but rather we will it in a qualified manner for the will is directed to things as they are in themselves, and in themselves they exist under particular qualifications. Hence we will a thing simply inasmuch as we will it when all particular circumstances are considered; and this is what is meant by willing consequently. Thus it may be said that a just judge wills simply the hanging of a murderer, but in a qualified manner he would will him to live, to wit, inasmuch as he is a man. Such a qualified will may be called a willingness (*velleitas*) rather than an absolute will (*absoluta voluntas*). Thus it is clear that whatever God simply wills takes place; although what He wills antecedently may not take place (*S.th.* I.19.6.*ad* 1).

One wills something *consequently* if one does in fact will it, that is to say, given Aquinas's identification of will with intellective appetite, if it is in fact the object of one's intellective appetite. And what one actually wills is of course willed *all things considered*. By contrast, one wills something *antecedently* if it is what one *would* will, other things being equal. One does not *actually* will something if one *only* wills it antecedently, not consequently. Strictly speaking, says Aquinas, we might better say that it is *willingness* rather than *will* that is involved. We do recognize it as a good; but before we actually will something, before we invest ourselves in its coming about, we must go beyond considering that good by itself and consider it along with "all particular circumstances."

Antecedent will—whether in God's case or ours—is thus a counterfactual state of affairs of a certain sort. It is what one *would* desire, or *would* be appetitively attached to, *were* the situation different in certain respects. God is not in fact appetitively attached to each and every person's being saved. Had things been different in certain respects, God *would* have been appetitively attached to that; specifically, had human beings not abused their free will, then God would have been appetitively attached to the salvation of all. But in actuality God is not appetitively attached to that; if God were, they would all be saved.

The application to the matter before us is this: sin is definitely out of accord with God's antecedent will, out of accord with God's willingness. But neither it nor anything else is out of accord with God's consequent will; that is to say, out of accord with what God actually wills. God's intellective appetite is always already satisfied. All natural evils are unavoidable components, conditions, or consequences of some greater good that God brought about. And all moral evils are permitted by God for the sake of some greater good, especially that of human free will. The reason there is no sorrow in God is—to say it again—that there is nothing for God to sorrow over.

The Import of Metaphorical Attributions of Passions to God

In the course of discussing the thesis that God loves all things, in *Summa theologica* I.20.2, Aquinas remarks that "Nothing prevents one and the same thing being loved under one aspect, while it is hated under another. God loves sinners in so far as they are existing natures; for they have existence, and have it from Him. In so far as they are sinners, they have not existence at all, but fall short of it; and this in them is not from God. Hence under this aspect they are hated by God" (*ad* 4). Doesn't this contradict the interpretation I have been developing? Doesn't God's hatred of the sinful act imply God's sorrowing over that act?

No, it does not. It is possible that Aquinas means to say only that the sinful act is out of accord with God's antecedent will. If so, that would remove any supposed contradiction. I think it far more likely, however, that Aquinas intends us to construe what he says here in the light of what he says about *metaphorical* attribution of affections to God.

In his *Summa contra gentiles* Aquinas noted that, given how Scripture speaks of God, it follows from what he has said concerning God's intellective appetite that "affections which in their species are repugnant to the divine perfection" are regularly predicated of God in Scripture (I.91.5). The clash is to be resolved by interpreting the predication "metaphorically" rather than "properly." Augustine had already developed the thought that the ground of such metaphorical attributions is "a likeness . . . in effects." Without mentioning Augustine, Aquinas embraces this principle of analysis, adding the qualification that in a few cases the ground may instead be "some preceding affection" (*ibid*).

Explaining the main line of analysis, Aquinas says that "the will at times, following the order of wisdom, tends to that effect to which someone is inclined because of a defective passion; for a judge punishes from justice, as the angry man punishes from anger. Hence God is at times called *angry* in so far as, following the order of His wisdom, He wills to punish someone, according to a Psalm (2:12): 'for his wrath is quickly kindled'" (*S.c.g.* I.91.16). In short, though there is no hatred or anger in God, God does sometimes do the sort of thing a human being would do out of anger; God does it out of love, however, not out of anger.

The same point is made in *Summa theologica*. After remarking, in the course of his discussion of God's will, that "some things are said of God in their strict sense; others by metaphor," Aquinas goes on to observe that "when certain human passions are predicated of the Godhead metaphorically, this is done because of a likeness in the effect. Hence a thing that is in us as a sign of some passion, is signified metaphorically in God under the name of that passion. Thus with us it is usual for an angry man to punish, so that punishment becomes an expression of anger. Therefore punishment itself is signified by the word anger, when anger is attributed to God" (*S.th.* I.19.11.*resp*). Notice: it is not *anger* that is signified by the word "anger" when attributed to God, but a certain act, viz., the act of punishment.

Concerning the qualification which he adds to the Augustinian line of analysis, Aquinas explains that

> I say *in some preceding affection* since love and joy, which are properly in God, are the principles of the other affections, love in the manner of a moving principle and joy in the manner of an end. Hence, those likewise who punish in anger rejoice as having gained their end. God, then, is said to be saddened in so far as certain things take place that are contrary to what He loves and approves, just as we experience sadness over things that have taken place against our will (*S.c.g.* I.91.17).

The point is this: just as we do not attribute anger and hatred to God on the ground of there being anger and hatred in God's life, so also we do not attribute sadness to God on the ground of there being sadness in God's life. In both cases, the attribution is metaphorical. The ground of the metaphorical attribution is different in the two cases, however. We metaphorically attribute anger and hatred to God on the ground of certain of God's actions resembling those actions which are characteristic of how human beings express anger and hatred; by contrast, we metaphorically attribute sorrow to God on the ground that some things take place which are contrary to what God loves and approves. We take the "preceding affection" of God's love—an affection which God does truly and properly have; we look to see whether anything goes contrary to it, since one sorrows for what goes contrary to what one desires; and if we find something of that sort, we metaphorically attribute sorrow to God. As we saw earlier, however, things go contrary only to God's antecedent will—to God's "willingness"—not to God's consequent will, that is, God's actual will. The ground of metaphorically attributing sorrow to God is the presence of something in the world that is contrary to God's antecedent will.

Is Aquinas's Defense Successful?

Has Aquinas successfully defended the claim that in God's life there is no sorrow, no sadness, no disturbance, nothing negative? The defense is undeniably subtle and profound. But is it successful? Has he borne the burden of proof?

A key component of Aquinas's defense is his distinction between God's antecedent and God's consequent will. It is natural to suppose that this distinction enables him to say that God *permits* a person to use his free will in a certain way while nonetheless *disapproving* of his using it thus, and *desiring that he not* do so. One thinks of analogies in human affairs. The father may disapprove of what his teenage son has done with his freedom, and desire that he not have done it, even though he thought that, all things considered, it was best to grant him freedom—and even though, in retrospect, it remains his judgment that it was best to grant his son freedom. The father decides to permit what he nonetheless disapproves of, and desires not to happen.

It is natural, I say, to interpret Aquinas's distinction as enabling him to say the counterpart thing for God: God permits us to do what

God nonetheless desires that we not do, and that God disapproves of our doing. But not so. Consider some act of torture. Unlike the parent's desire that the son not do what in fact he has done, God's antecedent will that the person not torture is not an *actual desire* on God's part. For one thing, if God actually desired that that person not use his freedom to torture another, that would be a frustrated appetite on God's part; but in Aquinas's theology, as we have seen, there is no room for frustrated appetite, no room for desire. Frustrated appetite yields sorrow; and in God there is no sorrow. Secondly, given Aquinas's identification of intellective appetite with will, if we attributed to God the actual desire (appetite) that that person not use his free will to torture, then some of what God actually wills would not come about; and that is unacceptable to Aquinas. For these reasons, merely antecedent will or appetite is not actual desire on God's part, to be distinguished from what God actually wills. In Aquinas's scheme, God does not actually desire that things be different from how they are; were that the case, there would be sorrow in God. In fact God is delighted with how things are.

Recall that antecedent will is a counterfactual truth of a certain sort. It is not the case that God wills that that person not torture; God is not in fact appetitively attached to that. What is rather the case is that had things been different in certain respects, then God would have willed that, would have been appetitively attached to it. And had that been the case, then the person would not have tortured.

Is this consequence of Aquinas's thought acceptable, the consequence that God is pleased with all that happens, that God disapproves of none of it, that God in no way desires that it be different? There will be some who will blurt out that were God like this, God would be an offense to their moral conscience, and will then stalk off, wishing to have nothing further to do with such a picture of God. That is also my view: Such a God would be an offense to my moral conscience, a conscience, let me immediately add, which has been shaped in its basic contours by Scripture. But I don't propose stalking off.

Recall the structure of my discussion here. I am not engaged in a project of natural theology; instead I am asking whether the philosophers and theologians of the Christian tradition, who *qua* Christian accepted the Christian Scriptures as canonical, had good reasons for holding that Scripture's representation of God as disturbed by humanity's waywardness and suffering is not to be taken as literally true. (As I mentioned earlier, one can ask the same question concerning the philosophers and theologians of the Jewish tradition.) When that is the project, there are always two considerations to keep in mind. The obvious consideration is whether a reason offered for holding that some aspect of Scripture's representation of God is not to be taken literally is sufficient for that purpose. Is the burden of proof successfully borne by the argument? A less obvious consideration is whether the reason offered, if true, undercuts the scriptural representation of God so deeply as to amount to a reason for holding that there just is no such God as Scripture represents. I doubt that it is possible to give a general description of the line between these two; one has to judge each case on its merits: Has the theologian or philosopher given sufficient reason for not regarding this aspect of Scripture's representation of God as literally true, while nonetheless not given sufficient reason for concluding that there is no such God as Scripture represents?

If God does not disapprove of humanity's waywardness and suffering, and does not desire that it be otherwise, then, so it seems to me, there just is no such God as Hebrew and Christian Scripture represents there as being; and if one *believes* that God does not disapprove of humanity's waywardness and suffering, nor desire that it be otherwise, then, whatever else one may do with these Scriptures, one will have to hold that in their representation of God they are misguided and mistaken at their very core. For at the very core of Scripture's representation of God is its representation of God as creating and redeeming. But if there is nothing in human affairs of which God disapproves, nothing that God desires to be otherwise, then redemption makes no sense. God sent Moses to lead Israel into a better land not on some divine whim but because God heard the cry of the people, knew their suffering, and desired that their affliction be alleviated.

I fully expect that not all readers will cozy up to this argument. So let me point out some further implications of Aquinas's thought. Aquinas appears to hold that God does actually and literally punish human beings for their wrong-doing. In one of the passages already quoted he says that since in human affairs it is usual "for an angry man to punish," the punishment being an "expression" of the anger, when Scripture attributes anger to God, "punishment itself" is to be understood as what is "signified by the word anger" (*S.th.* I.19.11.*resp*). The thought is pretty clearly that the reality which the word "anger" indicates, when predicated of God, is God's act of punishing the one with whom it is said, metaphorically, that God is angry. This interpretation is confirmed by Aquinas's remark, in another passage quoted earlier, that God wills "the evil of natural defect, or of punishment," by "willing the good to which such evils are attached" (*S.th.* I.19.9.*resp*).

Now I take it to be a conceptual truth that unpleasantness inflicted by one person on another is only *punishment* if the inflicter inflicts the unpleasantness because the other person (or someone intimately connected with him or her) has done something which the punisher *judges wrong*, and hence *disapproves of.* But on Aquinas's understanding of God, there is nothing which God judges wrong and hence disapproves of. There are indeed actions which God judges to be moral evils. But a moral evil, like all evils, is a departure from something's proper formation and functioning; and God does not judge, concerning evils, that they ought not to be, and, so does not—on the ground that they ought not to be—disapprove of them. All of them are required by, or a consequence of, or permitted for, some "greater good" which God wills. Though evils are contrary to God's antecedent will, none is contrary to God's consequent will, that is, God's actual will. Aquinas does connect punishment to moral evil; Aquinas remarks, again in a passage already cited, that though God antecedently wills all persons to be saved, God "consequently wills some to be damned, *as His justice exacts* (*S.th.* I.19.6.*ad* 1; italics added). But is it punishment if God imposes some unpleasantness on a person on account of that person's departure from proper functioning but does not judge that that functioning ought to have been otherwise, and accordingly, does not on that ground disapprove of that departure from proper functioning—nor indeed even desire that it not have occurred?

The same basic point can be gotten at from a different angle—I mean, the point that in Aquinas's picture of things there is nothing that is wrong, nothing that ought to be or have been otherwise. Let us approach the point by asking whether it is not an implication of Aquinas's thought that you and I should do what we can to eliminate sorrow from our lives, by eliminating all desire that things be otherwise than they are. For God sees things as they truly are, and in God's sight, all evils are required by, or permitted for, some greater good. Of course you and I discern at best a small piece of this cosmic pattern. But if one believes that this is indeed the pattern, isn't it right to do what one can to pattern oneself on God and eliminate all desire and sorrow, rather than allowing oneself to feel desire and sorrow as long as one does not oneself discern the way in which the evils serve some greater good?

I think Aquinas would deny that we should in this way seek to pattern ourselves on God. His reason can be inferred from his discussion of the question "whether sorrow can be a virtuous good" in question 39, article 2, of *Summa theologica* I-II. In his answer he first observes that he has already established that sorrow can be a good; the passage he has in mind is the one we quoted earlier, in which he observed that though sorrow is not as such a good, nonetheless sorrow over what is worth sorrowing over is an excellence in a person; in Aquinas's words, "sorrow is a good inasmuch as it denotes perception and rejection of evil." As to whether sorrow is a *virtuous* good, he then says this:

> These two things [perception and rejection of evil], as regards bodily pain, are a proof of the goodness of nature, to which it is due that the senses perceive, and that nature shuns, the harmful thing that causes pain. As regards interior sorrow, perception of the evil is sometimes due to a right judgment of reason; while the rejection of the evil is the act of the will, well disposed and detesting that evil. Now every virtuous good results from these two things, the rectitude of the reason and the will. Wherefore it is evident that sorrow may be a virtuous good.

The thought is this: sorrow, ensuing on the desire that things be otherwise, belongs to the proper functioning of human beings. The experience of sorrow upon stubbing my toe is a mark of proper functioning on my part; so too is the experience of sorrow over sin. After the passage quoted, Aquinas raises the question of whether it can be a virtuous good on our part to be opposed to sin when God, after all, permits it. His answer is that "a will that is opposed to sin, whether in oneself or in another, is not discordant from the Divine will" (*S.th*. I-II.39.2.*ad* 3). For nothing happens that is "discordant" from the Divine will, that is, from God's actual will, God's consequent will. Sin is not contrary to the divine will; sin is contrary to proper functioning. And very often it is proper functioning on my part to sorrow over improper functioning on your part—whether the evil in question be natural or moral.

But there is nothing anybody does that is wrong—nothing they do that they ought not to have done. Disapproval of some person's action on the ground that it is wrong is out of place. Human beings do indeed function improperly. But to observe that someone is functioning improperly is, so far forth, just to make a factual observation; it does not imply that what she did was *wrong*— that she *ought not* to have done it. After all, a rabbit functioning improperly is not doing anything wrong!

It is tempting to reply that improper functioning becomes something *wrong* when it is contrary to the divine will. But there isn't anything contrary to the divine will in Aquinas's scheme of things, not, to say it one more time, contrary to God's *actual* will.

And suppose one accepted the Thomistic picture: would not sorrow over sin, proper functioning though it be, soon disappear? If sins are not wrong, if they do not consist in doing what ought not to be done, if they are not contrary to the divine will—if they are nothing more than evils, that is, failures in proper functioning—then why sorrow over them? Except, of course, when they frustrate one's own desires. The virtuous good of sorrow over sin is seriously endangered by a Thomistic mentality.

My own conclusion is that it is the absence of the category of *the wrong* in Aquinas's picture of things that, above all, makes that picture unsatisfactory. The category of *the evil*, with which Aquinas operates, is simply a different category. Malformations and malfunctionings are not, so far forth, wrongs. And as to the traditional view, what makes something *wrong* is that it is contrary to the divine will: in Aquinas's picture of things there is nothing contrary to God's actual will.

Summary

Let us look back over the path we have travelled and ask what it was, at bottom, that led Aquinas to depart from Scripture's representation of God as disturbed by what transpires in the world. Was it perhaps his deep conviction that God is in no way deficient in excellence, coupled with the conviction that sadness represents a deficiency in excellence? Aquinas was indeed deeply committed to the first of these principles; but he himself said the right thing about the second: if there is something that calls for sadness on one's part, then it would not be an excellence but a *deficiency* in excellence were one not to experience sadness over that. Aquinas's departure from Scripture's representation proved instead to pivot on his conviction that there is nothing that transpires in creation which is contrary to God's intellective appetite; a conviction which, as we have seen, proves to have some extremely untoward implications in Aquinas's hands. But when we look back over this part of Aquinas's argumentation, it slowly dawns on us that he has offered no argument for the thesis that nothing happens that is contrary to God's intellective appetite; instead he has articulated an understanding of God *in the light* of that thesis.

What this shows, in my judgment, is that the deepest dynamic in the formation of the classical understanding of God proves ultimately not to be the thesis about God's excellence, important though that was, but rather the thesis concerning God's aseity. If the burden of proof is to be borne, for not regarding as literally true Scripture's representation of God as disturbed by what transpires in creation, it will have to borne by arguments drawn from God's aseity. But this is getting ahead of the story told in this paper. All I profess to have shown here is that Aquinas does not succeed in drawing from God's excellence a successful argument for the conclusion that God is not disturbed by sin and suffering, and that his way of articulating the thesis that God is imperturbably happy has some implausible, not to say, unsettling, consequences.

Endnotes

1.   Augustine explicitly accepts the principle in *de doctrina Christiana* III.10.14.

2.   I will be using the Dominican translation of the *Summa theologica*, and the translation by Anton C. Pegis of the *Summa contra gentiles*.

3.   The "first change wrought in the appetite by the appetible object is called *love*, and is nothing else than complacency (*complacentia*) in that object; and from this complacency results a movement towards that same object, and this movement is *desire*; and lastly, there is rest which is *joy*. Since, therefore, love consists in a change wrought in the appetite by the appetible object, it is evident that love is a passion: properly so called, according as it is in the concupiscible faculty; in a wider and extended sense, according as it is in the will" (*S.th*. I-II.26.2.*resp*).

4.   Though it will not play any role in my subsequent discussion, it is perhaps worth taking note of a distinction Aquinas makes between two kinds of sensitive appetite: *concupiscible* and *irascible* —"concupiscible" having the etymology of desire, and "irascible," that of anger. A concupiscible appetite is a desire for some good— this good in some cases being the aversion of some evil. An irascible appetite is then the desire to avert something which threatens one's enjoyment of that which is the object of a concupiscible appetite. The "irascible" is, as it were, "the champion and defender of the concupiscible, when it rises up against what hinders the acquisition of the suitable things which the concupiscible desires, or against what inflicts harm, from which the concupiscible flies. And for this reason all the passions of the irascible appetite rise from the passions of the concupiscible appetite and terminate in them . . . " (*S.th*. I.81.2.*resp*).

5.   *Cf. S.th*. I-II.24.2.*ad* 2): "In every passion there is an increase or decrease in the natural movement of the heart, according as the heart is moved more or less intensely by contraction and dilation; and hence it derives the character of passion."

6.   *Cf. S.c.g*. I.90.3: "it is manifest that joy or delight is properly in God. For just as the apprehended good and evil are the object of sensible appetite, so, too, are they of intellective appetite. It belongs to both to seek good and avoid evil. . . . There is the difference that the object of intellective appetite is more common than that of the sensitive appetite, because intellective appetite has reference to good and evil absolutely, whereas sensitive appetite has reference to good or evil according to the sense. So, too, the object of the intellect is more common than that of the sense. But the operations of appetite derive their species from their objects. Hence, there are found in intellective appetite, which is the will, operations that in the nature of their species are similar to the operations of the sensitive appetite, differing in that in the sensitive appetite there are passions because of its union to a bodily organ, whereas in the intellective appetite there are simple operations; for just as through the passion of fear, which resides in the sensitive appetite, someone flees a future evil, so without passion the intellective appetite does the same thing. Since, then, joy and delight are not repugnant to God according to their species, but only in so far as they are passions, and since they are found in the will according to their species but not as passions, it remains that they are not lacking even to the divine will."

7.   It is worth noting that Aquinas distinguishes two ways in which an act of appetite may "imply" an imperfection: the object of the act may be an evil, or, if the object is a good, one may be related to that good in an imperfect way. Hope is an example of the latter. This is what he says about why there is no hope in God: "the notion of the object of a given passion is derived not only from good and evil, but also from the fact that one is disposed in a certain way towards one of them. For it is thus that *hope* and *joy* differ. If, then, the mode itself in which one is disposed towards the object that is included in the passion is not befitting to God, neither can the passion itself befit Him, even through the nature of its proper species. Now, although hope has as its object something good, yet it is not a good already possessed, but one to be possessed. This cannot befit God, because of his perfection, which is so great that nothing can be added to it. *Hope*, therefore, cannot be found in God, even by reason of its species" (*S.c.g*. I.89.10).

8.   *Cf. S.th*. I-II.35.4.*resp*: "passions and movements, which derive their species from their terms or objects." Strictly speaking, the species of a passion, or of an act of intellective appetite, is determined not just by its object, but by its object plus the way in which the person is related to that object. See the preceding endnote.

9.   "Delight has the character of passion, properly speaking, when accompanied by bodily transmutation. It is not thus in the intellectual appetite, but according to simple movement: for thus it is also in God and the angels" (*S. th*. I-II.31.4.*ad* 2).